Improving
Communication
in the Library

Improving Communication in the Library

by Barbara Conroy and
Barbara Schindler Jones

ORYX PRESS
1986

The rare Arabian Oryx is believed to have inspired the myth of the unicorn. This desert antelope became virtually extinct in the early 1960s. At that time several groups of international conservationists arranged to have 9 animals sent to the Phoenix Zoo to be the nucleus of a captive breeding herd. Today the Oryx population is over 400, and herds have been returned to reserves in Israel, Jordan, and Oman.

Copyright © 1986 by The Oryx Press
2214 North Central at Encanto
Phoenix, Arizona 85004-1483

Published simultaneously in Canada

Printed and Bound in the United States of America

∞ The paper used in this publication meets the minimum requirements of American National Standard for Information Science—Permanence of Paper for Printed Library Materials, ANSI Z39.48, 1984.

Library of Congress Cataloging-in-Publication Data

Conroy, Barbara.
    Improving communication in the library.

    Bibliography: p.
    Includes index.
    1. Communication in library administration.
    2. Library administration—Staff participation.
    3. Library employees—Psychology.   I. Jones, Barbara S.
    II. Title.
    Z678.C745   1986   025.1   84-42815
    ISBN 0-89774-172-2

Contents

Preface

People everywhere struggle to improve their communication, knowing it is their lifeline to personal and professional success. Yet there is a special group of people, for whom this book is written, whose effective or ineffective communication affects ever-widening circles of other people and organizations. That group of people is librarians.

As librarians and library organizations ask for our consulting and training help, we are often told about a variety of communication problems. As we try to help solve these problems, it seems to us that librarians need to know more about *organizational* communication, and library directors need help in organizing and managing a *system* of organizational communication. Although "communication" is a frequent topic of discussion, of articles, and an occasional book, organizational communication is not included in most library school curricula, and rarely do staff development or continuing education programs include it. Consequently, little is available in library literature about organizational communication.

That is why *Improving Communication in the Library* has an organizational communication emphasis in which we look at channels and media and how messages move from unit to unit and level to level. Since interpersonal communication is obviously a part of the overall system, its important aspects are addressed as well. The main perspective we focus on is that of the library director or manager, yet the book is useful to all library staff because everyone in the organization contributes to and shares responsibility for organizational communication. When library personnel at all levels better understand how information, communication, and decision making interrelate and improve their communication skills, the library's overall effectiveness will be greatly enhanced, to the ultimate benefit of those they serve.

Throughout the book we have used the term "library" to refer to all types of libraries: public, academic and special libraries, and media centers. The book is also applicable to the growing number of information brokers and data specialists who work for business, industrial, educational, or non-profit organizations on a consulting basis or as permanent employees.

HOW THE BOOK IS ORGANIZED

Improving Communication in the Library has three major sections. Part I, "Organizational Communication in Libraries," introduces concepts that are used throughout the book, relating them specifically to internal and external communication in and from libraries and to the special problems of library managers. Part II, "People Working and Communicating Together," delineates specific communication skills required for interpersonal and group communication, and how they can be improved. Part III, "Communication and Change," prepares the librarian for the inevitable changes ahead, especially those brought about by our society's shift from an industrial to an information base.

ACKNOWLEDGEMENTS

We wish to thank the many librarians and library organizations whose concerns stimulated the writing of this book and especially those who so willingly gave ideas, insights, and suggestions. Their "real world" examples give depth and practicality to this book's content. For the first time in our experience, we do not have anyone to thank for typing the manuscript since the entire book was composed on our personal microcomputers, with the finished product transmitted directly to the publisher on disks. We find the symbolism as well as the reality of this new process particularly appropriate for a book about communicating in the information age.

Barbara Conroy
Barbara Schindler Jones

Part I
Organizational Communication in Libraries

Introduction

Organizational communication, as we use it in Parts I and II of this book, refers to a *human information system,* as opposed to the mechanical linkages provided by telephones and computers. This human information system contains both formal and informal channels for moving messages from unit to unit and level to level; words travel up, down, and laterally throughout the entire organization. Although there is obviously some overlap with interpersonal communication, the focus of organizational communication is more on the system itself and how it works than on person-to-person communication.

Designing and maintaining organizational communication has been called management's toughest job, yet it is apt to be handled more by default than by design. Top-level managers seldom involve themselves in the communication process as such; what's more, it is a rare library manager who understands the complexity of communication or who takes a "systems approach" in developing the library's communication patterns. Some large organizations have a "Director of Communication," but this person is seldom concerned with the organization's communication system. Rather, s/he is more apt to be involved with internal communication, such as with the organization's newsletters, or with external communication, such as with public relations and press releases.

Looking at a *system* of communication, as opposed to looking at specific memos or meetings, enables us to see that organizational design and consequent communication patterns vary according to scope and mission. What works in a hospital may fail in a bank; what works in one library may fail in another. Circumstances and ever-changing situations also affect an organization's communication system over time. Flexibility and adaptability are keys to developing an effective system.

THE CASE FOR MANAGING ORGANIZATIONAL COMMUNICATION

Letting communication within an organization "just happen" is not enough. Managers who follow a trickle-down theory ("We don't have to tell them—they'll find out through the grapevine") have abandoned their responsibilities. To be effective, organizational communication needs to be planned for, designed, executed, and evaluated. It needs to be purposeful, not inadvertent.

As Swartz wrote, "The 'information-sharing' level in an institution is a barometer of management's effectiveness with the staff. The cry of 'bad communications' comes only when the administrator is out of touch with the organization."[1]

Like water, communication will flow downhill on the path of least resistance. Planned communication, on the other hand, uses dams, channels, hydroelectric plants, as well as flood and drought control, to ensure that information gets to where it is needed and, at the same time, is diverted from places where it is not.

One of the most powerful skills the library manager can develop is the ability to communicate explicit information in the form that it is needed, at the time that it is needed, and without information overload. The manager with this skill doesn't just send out a memo and then sit back, confident that s/he has "communicated." This library manager checks to see if the message was read, and, if so, if it was clear, understood, believed, assimilated, accepted, and acted upon. And, if there was a problem with any of these aspects, this manager doesn't blame the recipient or "semantics." Instead, s/he immediately sets to work to correct and improve future transactions. Communication management is a task the manager cannot delegate.

A second equally powerful and equally important skill that a library manager needs in order to manage the library's organizational communication is the ability to obtain, as well as transmit, accurate and timely messages. Without this skill, the manager is cut off from data that are vitally important for decision making; at best, s/he will be forced to make decisions based on second- or thirdhand information.

A key point to remember is that effective organizational communication cannot be managed only by the people at the top of the organizational chart. Everyone in the organization has a stake in seeing that all of the other staff members get the information they need to do their jobs. When a system is being managed, all employees can and should be aware of how messages are sent and received and should be constantly on the lookout for ways to improve the system.

Part I explores those key roots of basic communication theory that apply to the library world. Examples show how both internal and external communication work in a variety of library situations, as well as their vital importance to the successful functioning of both managers and staff.

Chapter 1 lays the general groundwork for what is ahead. It highlights basic concepts and theoretical constructs for what occurs in communication generally and in organizational communication specifically.

Chapter 2 discusses the principal kinds and purposes of internal communication (messages that flow between levels, groups, and individuals within the library) and external communication (messages that flow between the library and its various publics).

Chapter 3 looks at organizational communication from a manager's perspective. Although everyone in the organization has responsibility for effective communication, managers have the overall authority for planning, managing, and evaluating all aspects of the communication that occur within or emanate from their organizations.

NOTE

1. Roderick G. Swartz, "Communications," in *Local Public Library Administration,* 2d. ed., ed. Ellen Altman (Chicago: American Library Association, 1980), p. 97.

Chapter 1
How Communication Occurs

Every living creature communicates. As human beings, we spend our lives surrounded by communication signs, signals, acts, and transactions. Messages abound. But not all messages are understood or consciously received. Not all messages are sent intentionally and many get "lost" en route. We know that most "people" problems can be traced in part or in full to poor communication, a "breakdown" in communication, or no communication at all. Human interaction succeeds or fails as a direct function of our ability to communicate. On the one hand, because every person communicates, it may seem unnecessary to define and explain the process. On the other hand, we seldom take time to wonder what actually happens when we try to transfer information, thoughts, and feelings even though giving and receiving all types of communication is such an integral (although largely subconscious) part of our lives. Our ability to communicate is so often taken for granted that we neglect to check for understanding; instead, we assume that we both understand and are understood in all instances.

Because the subject of communication is so broad and is interpreted in a variety of ways, we feel the need to select certain definitions and theoretical concepts that are particularly meaningful, in order to build a foundation for the rest of the book. It is our intention to extract the key concepts that most people could profit from understanding as well as those that apply most directly to the communication of librarians in all phases of their work. The following definitions and theories, therefore, are deliberately basic and introductory; they are not exhaustive in any sense. We hope that what is presented will stimulate the desire to learn more and motivate readers to do additional study on their own.

DEFINITIONS OF COMMUNICATION

Countless people from a variety of fields and disciplines have attempted to define communication. Some have given up after trying fruitlessly to encompass all potential variables. Others have given up when they realize that defining communication is difficult because it is not a finite product but a process. It is a dynamic, flowing, ever-changing phenomenon. Trying to understand communication is similar to trying to understand what a river is like by dipping out a bucket of water and studying it. In order to analyze or define communication, we must stop the very process that is its essence.

A broad, but useful, definition of communication as a whole is *all the procedures by which one mind affects another.*[1] Other acceptable definitions emphasize the *exchange* or *sharing* of information and the meeting of minds to achieve shared meanings that bring about *mutual understanding.*

Whenever we communicate, we deal with both content (the concept or attitude or emotion we wish to share) and process (how we try to transmit our message as well as the response we get or do not get). The person who believes that finding the right word or groups of words is the key to good communication misses the point of the importance of process. Putting the whole emphasis on content ignores two important factors—that (1) communication is an uncertain process because people make decisions that affect the outcome of any communication attempt and (2) messages may come from the outside (a speaker, a memo, or a television screen) but the meaning of those messages comes from within the person. Although messages can be transferred, meanings cannot. They are our own.

TWO MAJOR COMMUNICATION MODELS

Models are useful devices to illustrate what happens in the communication process. The two most frequently cited models are the linear and the cybernetic.

The Linear Model

Dating back to Aristotle, students of communication have used a static, linear model to describe how a message gets from its sender to its receiver. The components of the linear model that are usually identified are listed here. Each component has a vital role to play to ensure effective communication.

- Source: the individual, group, or organization that formulates a message (the encoder).

- Message: the stimulus produced by a source (anything has the potential of becoming a message).
- Channel: the means of transporting the message from the source to the receiver.
- Receiver: the person who gets, interprets, and reacts to a message (the decoder).

The Cybernetic Model

Norbert Wiener[2] is usually credited with developing the cybernetic model, which introduced the element of communication's effect, or as we identify it today, *feedback*. What happens as a result of the message? How does the message affect both the sender and the receiver? While the linear model places heavy emphasis on message construction, the cybernetic model adds the element of an adaptive control mechanism which makes the system dynamic and interactive. Following are two examples of the control mechanism at work.

A common illustration of the cybernetic system is the relationship between a thermostat and a furnace. The thermostat's message (temperature) "tells" the furnace to start producing heat; the heat produced "tells" the thermostat to change its temperature reading. Similarly, in the communication process, feedback to the sender permits the sender to change, improve, or correct the original message.

Another illustration in human terms is demonstrated by a crying baby. At first, new parents must rely on trial and error to interpret the meaning or need expressed by the crying, but it isn't long before parents can distinguish between different kinds of cries and adapt their behavior accordingly.

TWO MAJOR COMMUNICATION THEORIES

System Theory

Ludwig von Bertalanffy[3] and others designed the system theory. Among the theory's important tenets is that of *wholeness*. A system can be defined as an assemblage or combination of things or parts forming a complex or unitary whole, and the task of the systems analyst is discovering how the parts of a system are organized into the whole. Another tenet of systems theory is that of *structure*. Structure can be defined as sequences of communicative and other behaviors that are relatively constant and, to a certain extent, somewhat predictable, at least to members of the system.

When people comment that communication is the glue that holds organizations together, they are referring to system theory. System theory affirms the dynamic nature of communication. It takes into account the many organizational components and examines how they interact with one another. The key premise is that altering any single element or relationship will affect other elements and, thus, the whole.

Different disciplines have applied system theory in different ways. Communication specialists define a system as an identifiable social grouping in which individuals use communicative behaviors to form relationships and tie the group together. This definition, therefore, can encompass any group of people who live, work, or play together or who have some other reason to interact as a group. In library terms, a system can be anything from two people working together in the cataloging department to an entire network of libraries within a specific geographical area.

Information Theory

Information theory can be traced back to the study of electronic or machine-produced signals. From this background came the work of Claude E. Shannon[4] and others and the development of a mathematical theory of communication. Their focus is on message units (whatever could be measured and programed into a machine), not on message quality or the many variables that human beings can add to the system. As McGarry points out:

> One has to be clear at the outset that information theory is not a theory of information in the same sense that the term is used by the social scientist or the librarian; although there are many important comparisons which may be used, both to clarify the human communication process and the social function of librarianship.[5]

A key concept of information theory is *entropy,* which refers to randomness or unpredictability. Shannon and Weaver wrote that "information refers to knowledge that one does not have about what is coming next in a sequence of symbols."[6] Both order and redundancy are needed to reduce uncertainty. In his book *Grammatical Man,* Jeremy Campbell uses a library analogy to clarify the concept of entropy in different systems.[7] Campbell describes how a patron would try to find a copy of *War and Peace* in three libraries as follows: (1) in the first, each book has a unique catalog number and the book is in the fiction shelves, which are arranged in alphabetical order by the author's last name; (2) in the second, books are arranged on the shelves by the color of their bindings; and (3) in the third, the books are strewn at random on any shelf. In the first library, there is only one possible place that *War and Peace* could be arranged in relation to the other books. The order of the library provides the borrower with information, and uncertainty is low. In the second library, if the patron knows the color of the binding is red, s/he can go to the red section. The potential book borrower has less information about the order of the system and thus, s/he has more uncertainty. In the third library, the patron knows only that the book could be anywhere in the building and, therefore, his/her uncertainty is high.

The degree to which information eliminates ambiguity or confusion or the number of alternative possibilities reduces the information's entropy. High entropy means lack of knowledge and thus, uncertainty; low entropy means knowledge about the system exists and some degree of uncertainty has been removed.

Another example of entropy would be what happens when you have made arrangements to give a visiting dignitary a tour of your library, but on the scheduled day you receive a telegram saying, "Sorry. Missed 8 a.m. flight." Now you are confused. Is the person coming later? At all? What day? What time? Should you make duplicate arrangements? Very few alternatives were eliminated by the telegram. A far better message, which would eliminate most of the alternatives, would have been, "Sorry, arriving later than planned. Please reschedule tour for 3 p.m. today."

Since information theory developed as an engineer's model or as a control system, it includes the concept of "noise" or interference, such as the rustling of papers or static on the television. It also includes the concept that *redundancy* can be used to reduce errors. In this context, redundancy means more than just saying the same thing over again. Languages provide redundancy through their rules of syntax. For example, in English a pronoun must agree with its noun in gender, number, and case. People who know this rule can deduce the gender, number, and case of a noun even if some interference garbled the message.

THE ORGANIZATIONAL COMMUNICATION PROCESS

Whenever people gather in work or social settings, they develop interpersonal relationships that help them accomplish their objectives; they are said to have formed an organization. Organizations are primarily communication networks that vary according to the organization's size, scope, and function. Those who study organizations usually view them from one of four perspectives: (1) the classical theory, where the emphasis is on the shape of the formal organization to illustrate divisions of labor, functional differences, and spans of control; (2) the human relations model, which adds such human aspects as motivation and morale; (3) the social system or open systems school, which recognizes that all parts affect the whole and that the organization is influenced by factors outside as well as within the system; and (4) the industrial humanism perspective, which identifies participative management as the best way for an organization to survive in times of rapid change.[8] Although it is useful to understand these organizational perspectives, we need to remember that the distinctions between them may be rather arbitrary and there may be some overlap.

Despite the temptation to think of organizations as abstractions and to picture them as a pyramid of labeled boxes drawn on an official chart, we should focus on the fact that *organizations are people*—individual human beings linked together by communication. People, not labels or boxes, make organizations work, and they do so largely through communicating.

Why should organizational communication be a concern to a library or a library system? Because communication directly affects productivity, efficiency, morale, turnover, and public image, and because it is the primary means of accomplishing the work of the library: service to its patrons.

Networks and Systems

The arrangement or pattern of communication channels among the members of a group is known as a communication network (not to be confused with the grouping of libraries into a library network). An organization is, in its entirety, a communication network. Larger organizations are made up of many overlapping and integrating networks, which together make up the total organizational communication system.

People act as network nodes or magnetic centrals toward which messages are drawn and from which they emanate. Depending upon the individual's function, status, ability, and personality, some network nodes are more active and have a greater voice in the organization's operation than other nodes on the periphery. Traditionally, the "low one on the totem pole" may receive many messages but is permitted to initiate very few.

Communication networks in small groups can be delineated by observing the direction of message flow. In the principal patterns that are identified here (mainly through small group research), form not only follows function, but it is also reflective of leadership style.

Depending upon the size and objectives of the group, these different patterns have their places and purposes. The significance of understanding the variations is that group performance and individual satisfaction are affected by each person's centrality and access to the information necessary to do his/her job. People whose communication is restricted quickly realize that theirs is a limited position in which passively waiting for information to pass along is the expected and rewarded behavior. By contrast, people who work in an open channel network may be frustrated by the frequency and length of the many required meetings, but they certainly cannot complain about not being "in on things."

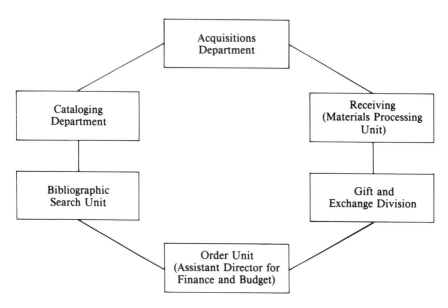

Figure 1. The Circle. Every member has equal opportunity to communicate and can communicate to the members on each side. Independence and flexibility, as well as satisfaction, are high. This network is more of a message circuit than a relay.

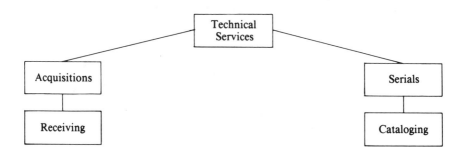

Figure 2. The Chain. The two people at the ends of the chain can communicate with only one other person. The mid-persons serve as relays along the chain from the end persons to the central position at the top.

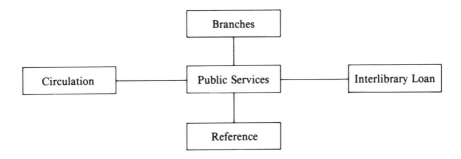

Figure 3. The Wheel. Considered the most structured of the networks, this pattern permits the people at the ends of the spokes to communicate only with the hub position. Two-way communication and feedback are discouraged because the hub person makes all decisions and relays them back.

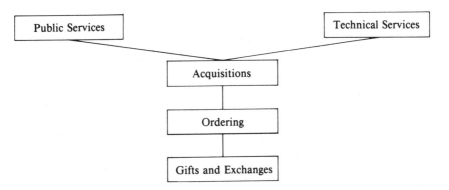

Figure 4. The Y. This pattern gives the most central person complete decision-making authority. The two people at the top are most apt to get information first.

In his experiments with small group communication networks, Leavitt found that the major behavioral differences attributable to communication patterns were differences in accuracy, total activity, satisfaction of group members, emergence of a leader, and organization of the group. There may also be differences among patterns in speed of problem solving, self-correcting tendencies, and durability of the group as a group.[9]

Lewis sums up the significance of communication networks in organizations when he points out that "these networks affect the behavior of individuals who work within them, and the position an individual occupies in the network plays a key role in determining his behavior and those he influences."[10]

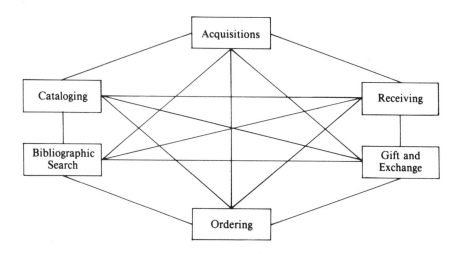

Figure 5. Open Channel. In this completely connected network, which is like the circle only with all points joined, there are no communication restrictions. Each person has access to everyone else; there is maximum feedback. Group satisfaction and morale are usually at their highest in this type of structure.

J. P. Wilkinson applies the research on small group networks to library settings and adds some of his own findings. He makes the point that libraries have neither adequately defined objectives nor have they matched tasks to behavior patterns. Further, Wilkinson advocates that a single communication pattern not be imposed on a library and that more complex objectives be carried out by highly participative structures and more routine functions follow restricted patterns.[11]

Formal and Informal Channels

The organization chart of your library, if it is in the traditional hierarchical form, probably traces the expected or *formal* channels of communication—who is supposed to talk to whom, who is supposed to tell what to whom, and who is supposed to report to whom. When messages follow the prescribed route, they are using the formal channels, usually a downward flow to subordinates or laterally to peers.

Informal channels indicate who really talks to whom, without regard to official position. Informal pathways are developed and shaped by such things as proximity (it is more convenient to talk to the person at the next desk), personal likes or attraction (people are more comfortable communicating with people they like), other relationships (the manager's husband is the maintenance person's cousin), and common values (person A and person B are from two different units but both are interested in improving the library's signage pattern). For these reasons, most organizations rely on a variety of informal linkages, as well as on powerful people who become information gatekeepers, to enhance the traditional, formal communication channels.

Communication Flow and Direction

People in different parts of an organization receive different kinds and amounts of information—and rightly and predictably so. Similarly, organizations with different purposes require different communication styles. As pointed out by Klauss and Bass,[12] free-flowing information may best serve an open organization with decentralized control (such as a hospital) while communication may need to be more organized and even tightly restricted in an organization requiring high control (such as a prison). Thus, information flow depends upon the goals, norms, and tasks of the organization and its subunits.

Overall, research that has quantified organizational communication and charted its direction reveals that, in most organizations, the bulk of communication is downward. Starting at the top of the typical hierarchical pyramid, messages flow down and fan out through the various levels in the form of memos, directives, and announcements. Although the dissemination of orders, policies, and plans is the backbone of most managerial communication, the one-way nature of most downward kinds of messages makes them less effective than interactive forms. Some managers see communication as a one-way street, with only themselves controlling the direction.

Next in frequency is information that is shared between peers. People at the same level communicate fairly frequently in both oral and written forms. Except for those possible instances brought about by such problems as interpersonal rivalry or separation in different locations, peer communication is usually informal, easy, and comfortable.

Least in frequency, and dropping off by a wide margin, is the kind of organizational communication that is intended to flow upward. Why is this? Is it true that no one wants to talk to the boss? Does the boss really want to know what's going on? Has the boss subtly indicated that s/he only wants to hear good news? Has the boss failed to reward upward communication efforts?

A principal value of upward communication is that it is the means by which managers can discover whether subordinates understand their messages. Meaning is clarified through feedback. If the channels are open—really open—and seen as such, potential misunderstandings are prevented. In addition, upward communication helps create a spirit of cooperation and teamwork. With good upward communication, managers can receive valuable ideas for planning and improving the organization and its operation. Since upward communication is not only a means of receiving "good" news, it can also serve to alert managers to problems which could, if not handled in time, develop into explosive situations which could definitely be bad news. Following are two examples of how upward communication can be inadvertently limited. One example is bureaucratic, the other attitudinal.

Suppose you are the public information officer in a large public library who is assigned to plan a long-range program to increase public awareness of library materials and services, but you have some questions about library policy to clarify before going ahead with your project. Normally, you would ask for an appointment with the library director, but a recent reorganization has added a layer of assistant directors to the library hierarchy. You are told to see the assistant director for public services instead. But the problem is complex, the discussion is long. At its conclusion, the assistant director says, "The director will have to make that decision." Hours have been wasted because your attempt to communicate upward was blocked, and you have been kept one level away from the person able to solve your problem or take the action you need.

In the second example, suppose you are the assistant director for public services, and you have a long list of items to discuss with the library director. You are aware that the director has been under stress, working long hours because of severe, unforeseen problems. Because you don't want to add to the director's burdens, you eliminate several problems from your list to discuss, deciding to postpone some and handle others yourself. With the best of intentions, you have cut back on the amount of upward communication you normally would provide.

It is easy to believe that the lack of upward communication means that all is well. But no news is not necessarily good news. Effective managers who are aware of the value of organizational communication don't wait for upward communication to reach them; they "walk the shop," they watch and listen, and, above all, they appreciate and reward any and all forms of upward communication. Chapter 3, "Special Concerns of Library Managers," describes in more detail how library managers can increase their supply of upward communication.

Another aspect of communication flow that needs to be monitored is accuracy. There is a direct correlation between the number of people through whom messages must be relayed and the amount of distortion that occurs. Even intelligent, well-meaning staff members hear and transmit different parts of the same message. Each person abstracts from the total message through different interest and value screens. They grasp and retain only what makes sense to them and what appears to be relevant to their needs and concerns. Studies of communications that have filtered through several layers of organizational structure show that even good news changes by the time it reaches the lowest level. Organizations that have staff members in different locations, as well as at different levels, have an especially difficult time ensuring that people get full and accurate information.

In situations where organizational communication is managed, attention is paid to the key roles served by "linking-pins" in the organization. This idea, originated by D. C. Pelz and developed by Rensis Likert[13] identifies those individuals who are members of more than one group and thus, serve as natural communication conduits to improve overall communication flow. An example of a linking-pin would be the manager of a subunit who is also a member of a group of middle managers who regularly meet with an assistant director. Linking-pin positions, when filled by aware and skilled people, can keep channels open for both downward and upward communication. Obviously, people who are not skilled or who don't assume responsibility for the transmission of information can cause severe breakdowns in the library's internal flow of information.

THE EFFECTS OF ORGANIZATIONAL STRUCTURE ON COMMUNICATION

Many organizations put a lot of time and effort into devising and revising their organizational charts. Although staff members can certainly profit from knowing how their roles and functions fit into the overall scheme, perhaps too much attention has been focused on orderly boxes and not enough upon the communication that takes place between the boxes. As a substitute for real problem solving, many organizations have adopted the policy "When all else fails, we can always reorganize!"

Most library managers know that no organizational structure works merely because it is well-designed and looks good on paper. They know from experience that the organizational system works well only if the people represented by the little boxes give their best efforts and have faith in the system. A typical, traditional organizational chart might look like this.

Vertical hierarchies are based on the assumptions that (1) organizations function by passing information upward through management levels, while decisions and orders based on this information are passed back down; (2) the "brain" of the organizational body is at the top, and it does all of the decision making on important matters; and (3) organizational levels correspond to competence so that the higher the person is in the structure, the more skilled and dedicated s/he is. These assumptions are sometimes valid, sometimes not.

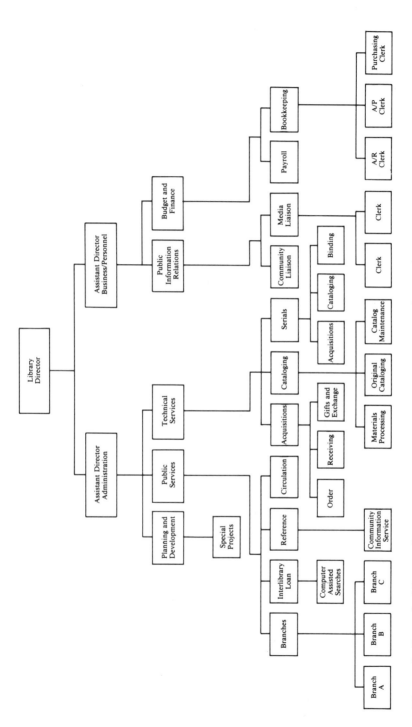

Figure 6. Generic Library Organization. A composite, generic chart that blends several actual library structures that are arranged in the typical hierarchical pyramid.

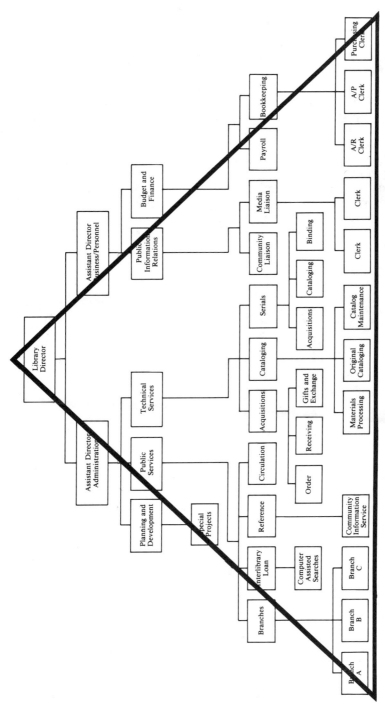

Figure 7. Modified Generic Library Organization. Includes the pyramid to highlight this type of organization structure, with a few people (top managers) at the top, a few more (middle managers) in the middle, and the bulk of the work force at the bottom.

Some organizations, distressed to find that their structure cannot fit into a pyramid, worry about being different or wrong. The important point to keep in mind is that organization charts are drawn to show relationships and intersecting functions—in short, the picture of reality for that group. People (and their symbolic boxes) should *not* be arranged to fit some stereotypical notion of what an organizational chart is supposed to look like. Once freed from the mandate of a pyramid, organizational managers can depict imaginative designs to reflect how the structure actually works without the worry of whether it is orthodox or not.

As an example of this, a group of scientists realized, with the help of consultants, that their organizational structure looked more like a daisy than a pyramid. In this form, shown in Figure 8, the petals represent individual, overlapping research teams, where each team is loosely connected to two other teams. The center disk represents the administrative staff, which serves all of the teams and coordinates them.

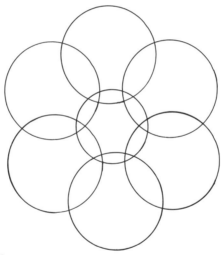

Figure 8. The Daisy.

Stueart and Eastlick describe a library organization pattern which is shaped like a doughnut, one in which the chief administrator resides in the hole and all of the services and subunits are placed in successive circles.[14] Another design mentioned by Stueart and Eastlick and widely adopted by many organizations is the matrix pattern which allows the formation of special groups for special purposes.[15] For example, temporary task forces might be formed by making lateral slices across separate, autonomous units (such as choosing the managers of several units or departments to form their own group) or by selecting representative individuals from a variety of departments or levels (such as asking each unit or department involved to select or elect a representative to serve on a separate task force).

Although chances are the hierarchical pyramid will be around for a long time, it is clearly less pervasive in contemporary organizational structures than it once was. As organizations grow and become top-heavy, the growth falls in on itself and the top of the pyramid collapses, as indicated in Figure 9. The result is increased decentralization.

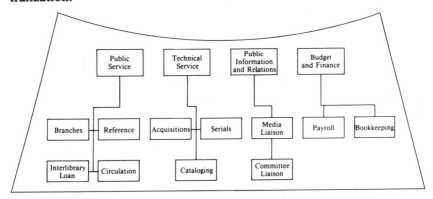

Figure 9. Collapsed Pyramid.

In his book, *Dismantling the Pyramid,* Paul Von Ward identifies some of the major problems with cumbersome, pyramidal bureaucracy as institutional lethargy, demotivation, interpersonal defensiveness, personnel mismatches, and game playing.[16] He points out that too many people believe that "a few good people can make the system work," which explains why each new wave of officials arriving in Washington, DC, blames government chaos on their predecessors.

Another writer who foresees a shift away from hierarchies to networks is John Naisbitt. In his popular book, *Megatrends: Ten New Directions Transforming Our Lives,* Naisbitt predicts that the pyramid power structure, in which people at the top give orders to people at the bottom, will be replaced by a network of people talking to one another and sharing ideas, information, and resources.[17]

Instead of conducting business through vertical systems, increasing numbers of organizations are working in spirals or circles (as in the doughnut scheme) or sideways or crossways (as in the matrix pattern). In this age of increasing specialization, competence is no longer found exclusively at higher levels. Rather, it is more likely found scattered throughout an organization. This factor takes on even more significance with the advent of sophisticated technology in the electronic library. While writing about the burgeoning of technology in the work place, Daniel Goleman quoted social psychologist Shoshana Zuboff as saying:

We are likely to see a gradual shift in the overall shape of the organization from a pyramid to something closer to a diamond shape, with a diminishing clerical support staff, swelling numbers of professionals and middle managers, and a continually more remote, elite, policy- making group of senior managers.[18]

The library manager who wants to improve the organization's communication must first thoroughly understand the library's real (not paper) structure. The following questions may help you understand the structure more clearly.

- Through what formal and informal paths do staff members get the information they need to do their work?
- Do unit leaders have to base their decisions on second- or thirdhand information rather than firsthand knowledge?
- Does the structure create barriers that virtually isolate upper-level personnel?
- Are there unused or clogged channels in the system?
- Would rearranging people and/or tasks to phase out some aspects of an outmoded hierarchy improve productivity and morale?

There is no doubt that an organization's structure has a profound influence on its communication, but the reverse may also be true—communication processes may also determine structure. Certain informal relationships and patterns may eventually become formalized and made a part of the structure.

ORGANIZATIONAL BARRIERS TO COMMUNICATION

In addition to the barriers created by the organizational structure itself, the chief cause of other barriers can be summed up in one word: bureaucracy. Some organizations have been led by individuals with bureaucratic mind-sets for so long that the thought of changing the system can be compared to trying to run through a vat of molasses. That kind of organization is one where paper is more important than people and where process is more important than the organizational mission. Out of frustration and boredom, people become masters at "looking busy," and to protect their jobs, people expand the "necessary" paperwork and already tedious rules and regulations.

Harry Cohen described a painfully bureaucratic library that had 22,000 new books that no one could touch since a cut in appropriations had led to insufficient staffing in the cataloging department. Despite the fact that numerous idle employees in other departments complained about not having enough to do and volunteered to help, 22,000 books remained uncataloged and unshelved. Why? Because the personnel manager told workers he would "get back to them," but he actually did nothing. To compound the problem, the heads of the overstaffed departments wouldn't "spare" workers for fear this would show them to be poor delegaters. Cohen concludes the sad tale as follows.

> Soldiering is something that is not confined only to the army. It is the process of doing it their way, making a good show of heel clicking, and letting someone else worry about the results. It's coming to the realization that everything is snafu and that it can even be fun contributing to that snafu.[19]

True, bureaucracies are formed and maintained by people, but once instituted, the bureaucratic system seems to take on a life of its own, independent of the people struggling to modify it. It is for this reason that we term bureaucracy an organizational barrier rather than a human one.

Another organizational barrier occurs because of the sheer amount of communication activity. People are bombarded all day, every day, with attempts to influence what they do, think, feel, or buy. As a result, our responses are numbed. Blind eyes and deaf ears make us no longer receptive to receiving and passing along information. Ries and Trout, in their book, *Positioning: The Battle for Your Mind* use the following metaphor.

> The average mind is already a dripping sponge that can only soak up more information at the expense of what's already there. Yet we continue to pour more information into that supersaturated sponge and are disappointed when our messages fail to get through.[20]

Communication overload is a real problem. What organizations need is not *more* communication but *better* communication.

HUMAN BARRIERS TO COMMUNICATION

The number of human failings that cause barriers in organizational communication is probably limitless. Five of the most troublesome of these barriers are described here.

Personality Differences

When people work together, they bring with them their own unique personalities with individual attitudes, beliefs, values, and needs. In addition, each has his/her own unique communication style and temper flash point. By taking just one aspect—value differences—as an example, we can see how the library's communication can be impeded. If an assistant director highly values the control of information and uses it as a source of power, selected people and work units may receive early information about planned changes or hints of problems on the rise, while other people on the same assistant director's staff become frustrated or apathetic from being left out of such communications. Another manager, on the other hand, may value full and open communication for all of his/her staff, with the result that this manager's team approaches their work with a very different, more positive attitude.

Since unique personalities are a given, managers learn, as a fact of organizational life, that it is hopeless to try to change anyone's basic personality or value system. It is better to use the energy to place employees so that their personalities, as well as skills, suit the tasks they are to perform. To some extent, intentional team building very often helps staff members understand and appreciate each other's special qualities, thereby reducing interpersonal conflict.

Perception

How each person sees the world and makes sense of it is linked to personality as well as past experience. It has been said that every frog sees the world from its own puddle of water. People also see the same phenomenon and its various aspects differently. Communication can be significantly affected by this unconscious selective perception process. How people perceive a problem and their role in it determines how they will communicate about it, what they will decide, and how they will act. If the head of the reference department proposes a new project for the library, s/he may not understand why it fails to get off the ground unless the assistant director communicates to her that it was not the project that was unsound but rather that it was perceived to be too expensive to implement.

Low Self-Esteem

A significant human barrier to communication is low self-esteem. Our self-esteem is the result of the reputation we build within ourselves; it involves our perception and our personal feeling of worth, lovableness, and capability. Positive self-esteem leads to clear thinking and results in unclouded messages and unblocked listening.

Our own thoughts create our feelings; feelings are not caused by other people, circumstances, or the weather. Individuals with low self-esteem frequently use blame or justification to steer their own thinking process, thus making them happy or sad, positive or negative.

Of course, a supervisor cannot successfully tell an employee to raise his/her self-esteem. However, by being alert to the barrier of low self-esteem, managers can take it into account and provide as much positive feedback as possible to strengthen a staff member's sagging self-esteem.

Lack of Communication Skills

High on this list is the lack of *listening* skills. People often hear what they expect to hear and often stop listening altogether while they mentally frame their next comment. Writer Rebecca West has been credited with the remark: "There are no real discussions any more, only intersecting monologues." A significant part of the communication process is the need for meaning clarification. "Semantics" is frequently blamed for many miscommunications. Yet what else do we have but words (and their accompanying nonverbal clues) with which to communicate? When people assume understanding and believe that because they have spoken they have communicated, they forget that words only have meaning in terms of how people define them. Clarifying and sharing meanings are twin goals of communication. For too many people, however, these skills are underdeveloped.

Attitudes about Communication

Individuals in visible positions within an organization communicate something about themselves and their organization whether they intend to or not. Sometimes managers believe that they control what is communicated; they believe that if they choose to withhold information, others will remain uninformed. Such managers forget that silence in itself communicates a message and that people have access to many other sources of information.

The staff member who does not take responsibility to initiate and respond to communication, believing it is someone else's job, creates barriers that can affect the entire organizational system. The library director who hoards information, believing that others in the system do not need or do not have the right to what s/he considers to be private and privileged data, also creates a barrier. Candor and trust are essential for clear and effective communication. People who are kept in the dark about information they need to do their work soon find other means of getting what they need, or they give up trying and do without, which means they are trying to work with a severe handicap.

Another dangerous attitude about communication is held by the person who feels messages should impress rather than express. This form of deliberate noncommunication—obfuscation, jargon-happy discourse—is often a large, unchallenged barrier. Although all professions and businesses develop their own specialized jargon and acronyms which can be used to shortcut lengthy explanations, the danger comes when staff members no longer recognize the difference between jargon and common usage. Outsiders sometimes suspect that the jargon is used to exclude rather than communicate. Libraries and other educational institutions seem particularly prone to this syndrome. James C. Thompson, an associate university librarian, explains this with regard to libraries.

> No two libraries operate in quite the same way, and no two librarians use the same words to describe what they do, even within one library. It would be hard to get even a small group of librarians to agree on the usage of such common terms as serial, series, periodical, continuation, or analytic. . . The professor who wants a new book and is told "we could firm-order that as a do-not-duplicate under our approval profile, but if it's a continuation it should come on standing order" is liable to give up on the library as well as the book.[21]

Attitudes about What a Library Is and How It Should Be Operated

It comes as no surprise that library goals and philosophies vary widely. Communication barriers can arise when work groups do not take the time to discuss, clarify, accept, or act on organizational and department goals. All too often, old-timers who have internalized goals and objectives take them for granted, forgetting what it is like to be a new member of the team who is unclear about what the group is working toward.

What is the library for? To catalog and preserve books? To impart knowledge? To be a repository for the world's knowledge? Serve the community? Solve problems? All of the above? Differences in the vision of a library can skew its services and functions and can present a barrier to effective communication. Complete, mindless conformity is not the answer. What is needed is the kind of cohesion and teamwork that puts the needs of the organization ahead of individual visions and concerns. Similarly, the organization's need for full, honest, and timely information must supersede any one individual's divergent view.

Conclusion

These barriers are common in organizational situations—so common, in fact, that we often fail to take them into account as we cope with daily routines and crises. Many work problems are caused by, or intensified by poor communication habits. We must be alert to these problems and willing to understand that a coworker's perceptions, attitudes, and self-esteem are important at all staff levels. A reminder to ourselves and others about inappropriate use of jargon can also be useful. Taking considerate initiative to improve understanding and communication with others builds bridges for more effective organizational communication.

NOTES

1. Claude E. Shannon and Warren Weaver, *The Mathematical Theory of Communication* (Urbana, IL: University of Illinois Press, 1949), p. 3.

2. Norbert Wiener, *Cybernetics: Or Control and Communication in the Animal and the Machine* (New York: John Wiley & Sons, 1948).

3. Ludwig von Bertalanffy. "General System Theory—A Critical Review," in *Modern Systems Research for the Behavioral Scientist,* ed. Walter Frederick Buckley (Chicago: Aldine Publishing Company, 1968).

4. Claude E. Shannon, "A Mathematical Theory of Communication," *The Bell System Technical Journal* 27 (1948): 379–423.

5. Kevin McGarry, *Communication, Knowledge and the Librarian* (London: Clive Bingley Ltd., 1975), p. 21.

6. Shannon and Weaver, p. 103.

7. Jeremy Campbell, *Grammatical Man* (New York: Simon and Schuster, 1982).

8. See Thomas R. Tortoriello, Stephen J. Blatt, and Sue DeWine, *Communication in the Organization* (New York: McGraw-Hill Book Company, 1978), pp. 25–44; and Edgar Huse and James Bowditch, *Behavior in Organizations* (Reading, MA: Addison-Wesley Publishing Co., 1973), pp. 42–43.

9. H. J. Leavitt, "Some Effects of Certain Communication Patterns on Group Performance," in *Organization Theory,* ed. D. S. Pugh (New York: Penguin Books, 1971), p. 97.

10. Phillip V. Lewis, *Organizational Communications: The Essence of Effective Management* (Columbus, OH: Grid, Inc., 1975), p. 42.

11. J. P. Wilkinson, "The Psycho-Organizational Approach to Staff Communication in Libraries," *The Journal of Academic Librarianship* 4 (1) (1978): 21–26.

12. Rudi Klauss and Bernard M. Bass, *Interpersonal Communication in Organizations* (New York: Academic Press, 1982), p. 32.

13. Rensis Likert, *New Patterns of Management* (New York: McGraw-Hill, 1961).

14. Robert D. Stueart and John Taylor Eastlick, *Library Management* (Littleton, CO: Libraries Unlimited, 1977), p. 68.

15. ———, p. 69.

16. Paul Von Ward, *Dismantling the Pyramid* (Washington, DC: Delphi Press, 1981).

17. John Naisbitt, *Megatrends: Ten New Directions Transforming Our Lives* (New York: Warner Books, 1982). See also William A. Kraus, *Collaboration in Organizations: Alternatives to Hierarchy* (New York: Human Sciences Press, 1980).

18. Daniel Goleman, "The Electronic Rorschach," *Psychology Today.* 17 (2) (February 1983): 36–43.

19. Harry Cohen, "The Tin Soldiers of Bureaucracy," *Management Review* 61 (4) (April 1972): 3–9.

20. Al Ries and Jack Trout, *Positioning: The Battle for Your Mind* (New York: Warner Books, 1981), p. 7.

21. James C. Thompson, "Advanced Library Obfuscation, or The Modifiable Ergonomic Dimensions of the English Language," *American Libraries* 15 (3) (March 1984): 138–42.

Chapter 2
Organizational
Communication and Libraries

Library communication is of two specific and basic types— internal and external. Although overlap may exist between these two kinds of communication, as when the same memo or announcement is distributed both inside the library and to people or groups outside the library, distinctions should be made between the two.

INTERNAL COMMUNICATION

Communication internal to an organization includes those messages that flow among levels, groups, and individuals within the library. As described in Chapter 1, these messages may be directed downward, upward, or laterally, or they may move through networks of many different configurations. Everyone in an organization needs information in order to make intelligent decisions and solve problems, thus, the library that provides effective communication to all its members also provides itself and its workers the best environment for production and worker satisfaction.

The focus of internal communication should be on what library staff want and need to know. Typically, staff members want to know such things as how the library is organized, how it functions, what policies are in effect (especially new policies that affect them), and how their jobs fit into the organizational scheme. Most important, of course, is the steady flow of information staff members need in order to do their jobs efficiently and effectively. Likewise, managers want and need information from all staff levels. Meltzer describes a graphic image in *The Information Imperative.*[1] He pictures an organizational wheel with two kinds of forces: those flowing toward and those flowing away from the hub of top management where "centrifugal communication flows away from the hub in the form of policies, decisions, strategies, and directives. But where the information flows outward to be acted on, it is based on incoming data that enter the organization as a centripetal force."[2]

As has already been stressed, effective communication needs to be two-way and interactive, thus making listening and feedback key elements in all internal communication. Everyone shares in the task of making communication work, yet the ultimate responsibility for ensuring that the right kind and amount of information is disseminated to the right people in a timely way obviously belongs to the library director (or his/her designee). Where organizational communication is managed and standardized, planned distribution of information supplants a random, haphazard information flow.

One example of managing information flow is the Selective Dissemination of Information (SDI) that routes only information based on the user's field-of-interest profile. This changes the random pattern to a planned one, offering the advantage of consistency but the disadvantage of loss of serendipity. Long used in special and academic libraries for serving clientele needs, a similar scheme can also be effective internally.

Library managers and staff are not the only senders and receivers of the library's internal communication. Many libraries also have volunteers and a board of directors or trustees. Although library users are not an official part of the library's organizational structure, they are important senders and receivers of internal communication also.

Purposes of Internal Communication

These are the principal reasons people communicate within the library.

- To inform: convey both information and understanding.
- To gather information: collect input from others to help make decisions and solve problems.
- To motivate: change or reinforce behavior, to prompt specific action.
- To persuade: "sell" ideas, products, or services to others.
- To instruct and/or train: enable another to carry out instructions, tasks, or procedures appropriately.
- To coach and/or discipline: foster growth and prevent disciplinary action, to help another learn how to do a specific task better, improve attitudes or behavior.
- To counsel: help someone with a personal problem that affects work productivity or morale.
- To mentor: help another succeed, usually by imparting a better understanding of organizational policies, practices, or politics.
- To develop staff: guide staff progress and growth with performance appraisals and goal-setting sessions.
- To build teams: help work groups establish interpersonal rapport, build esprit de corps, and develop cohesion.

To Inform

Since people need information in order to do their jobs, informing is perhaps the most central and common function of internal communication. When library personnel attempt to "spread the word," their purpose is one or all of the following: to tell people something they don't know, to give meaning to facts they already know, or to clarify and expand upon information previously dispensed. This seems like a simple process if we believe that talking and telling or writing are all that are required; giving out information is only a part of the process, however. We have already stressed the importance of interaction, response, and feedback to bridge the gap between merely receiving information and being able to understand it and use it. To be useful, new information must be understood by recipients in terms of what it relates to and how, as well as what it has to do with them.

Thus, the sender of information can never merely pass it out; the sender must see that the receiver gets it in a way it can be used. The purpose and relationship to the receiver need to be made clear at the very beginning rather than be buried somewhere in the middle. The sender must organize information into meaningful groupings. Specific, concrete points are more useful than vague and abstract information; long and more involved material requires frequent summaries. Since people can absorb and remember only so much, interestingly presented information aids motivation, understanding, and retention.

To Gather Information

Most experienced managers recognize that gathering information is a two-way street and that upward communication is just as important as downward communication. Gathering information from staff, whether it be in the form of suggestions, gripes, attitudes, or opinions, provides indispensable input for management decision making. What's more, effective information gathering can assess and improve employee morale.

But some managers have difficulty recognizing and clearing away barriers to allow useful and honest messages to come up through the hierarchy. "How do staff members *really feel* about the new health and accident plan?" seems a simple enough question, but the answer may be amazingly elusive. Managers who consistently nurture a supportive, cooperative organizational climate will find upward communication to them increasing in volume and improving in quality. Two questions managers must frequently ask of themselves are: "Do I really want to know what is going on and how the staff feel?" and "Do I really want to hear the bad news as well as the good?"

Staff at all levels, including managers, gather information as a matter of course. Mostly, this is through informal means such as questioning individuals on a one-to-one basis, referring to the library's procedural manuals, or reading bulletin boards. Some individuals are more purposeful than others about information- gathering efforts: They identify what they need to know with more precision, target the sources of that information, and persist until they get what they need to know.

Many people "mine" interviews, meetings, and coffee breaks for what they need to know. Depending upon the overall climate, as well as interpersonal skills, face-to-face methods can be highly useful or very threatening to staff members. To counteract the potentially threatening aspect, some libraries have newsletters, grievance systems, personnel counselors, and ombudspersons as additional formal sources for staff input.

Managers can also use more formal methods to gather information on a wider scope. Opinion polls (a sampling or collection of opinions on a subject, taken from either a selected or random group of persons) and attitude surveys (a sampling of attitude on a given subject taken and used to approximate or indicate what a complete collection and analysis might reveal) are commonly used, particularly in large organizations. Though not used often in libraries, they can bring problems to the surface, assess opinions, and open channels of communication. The quality of surveys is influenced by organizational climate, patterns of staff participation, and accustomed levels of trust and openness.

Constructing both useful and valid instruments isn't easy. Many survey questionnaires have been scrapped by their authors only after they discovered, the hard way, that poorly framed questions elicited ambiguous answers; that answers to open-ended questions could not be adequately quantified; or that the 30-percent response rate did not provide a valid cross section of opinion.

Survey responses are not always honest. Even if pleased to be asked, staff may suspect a gimmick or hidden agenda. Insecure people may think honest, but negative, answers will put their jobs on the line. Even highly competent, totally secure workers may give biased answers out of loyalty to the library and/or supervisor. How can managers get accurate and useful upward communication via surveys? First, the process should be part of the regular communication flow and not a sudden, special project; a survey should be only one of many methods used to gather information.

No matter which method for upward communication is used, staff members must be assured that whatever information is volunteered will not be used against them. Moreover, they need to know that the information supplied is important to management, that it will make a difference, and that it will be used in decision making. Willing participation in such activities will decrease if it becomes obvious that management has no intention of correcting the problems uncovered. Few employees are fooled by propaganda circulated under the guise of questionnaires or surveys.

Here are some suggested steps to follow when conducting polls or surveys.

1. *Define and clarify objectives.* The purpose of the survey should be clear to those involved with it; they should understand and agree on its purposes. What is the survey to disclose? Will straight information or opinions or both be solicited? Generally, polls are used to gather information that does not readily flow upward through usual channels. Could these channels be cleared instead of taking a survey?

2. *Target the audience.* Will the survey be administered throughout the library (including branches or other units) or will the people chosen be part of a narrow, select group? Depending on the library's size, a sample population may provide the information needed if it is truly representative of the larger group.

3. *Pretest.* Pilot polls conducted among small samples of the target group will save time and money in the long run. They can uncover weaknesses in the proposed questions, the form, the procedures, or the compilation methods. A pretest will point up slanted questions or indicate if a questionnaire is too long.

4. *Finalize the form and format.* An opinion poll usually starts with questions about the employee, such as age, sex, and length of service. The next block of questions may be in an agree/disagree format, multiple choice, items to rank, checklists, or open-ended questions. The format should be designed to make the survey a clear and convenient instrument to help the respondent. The survey itself is a communication and can serve as a motivating factor.

5. *Decide how best to administer the survey.* Depending on the size of the organization and its geographical spread, choose between (a) a mail survey to be sent to the office or home or (b) assembling staff in one location to answer the questions.

6. *Analyze and disseminate results.* The manager or designee needs to know how to handle statistical formulas, analyses, and procedures that can turn raw data into meaningful information. Has the instrument been tested for validity to make sure it measures what it is supposed to? Decisions also must be made on the best means of broadcasting or distributing the results. Should they be presented in narrative, statistical, or graphic form, or a combination? Are summaries adequate or is complete detail better?

7. *Plan for administrative follow-up.* Who will review the data and decide what they mean and what needs to be done? Is corrective action necessary? Should policies be changed?

What would be the best time and method to inform all affected personnel?

If these seven steps seem too complicated or time-consuming to follow, consider having an impartial outside individual or agency administer a survey instead. Larger organizations, particularly, will find a professionally done survey more objective as well as more time- and cost-effective.

To Motivate

The theory of motivation is much more complex than the simple (and simple- minded) notion that people are motivated in only two ways: the carrot or the stick (incentive or punishment). Motivation is a set of complex, interacting forces that come from within, rather than from any method or technique that other people "do" to us or use on us. These internal forces are often called needs, and attempts to satisfy needs are what prompt people to think and act and are, therefore, what motivates them. Individual motives can rarely be really understood by others. They are complicated and highly personal and often a mystery even to the person driven by them.

Rizzo points out that there are many different ways to interpret what managers mean when they say they have a worker "who isn't motivated."

> One manager would mean that people do not take initiative . . . Another manager . . . that they do not seem to react appropriately when problems arise. A third might mean that employees do not care about their work, the organization, or personal career advancement. A fourth may be reacting to low productivity or qualitatively poor work. A fifth might be saying that the organization is failing to provide adequate incentives to employees. Still others might have a different basis for their comment, such as a conclusion that employees are dissatisfied.[3]

Library managers are undoubtedly familiar with the major motivation models such as Maslow's hierarchy of needs,[4] Locke's goal-related behavior,[5] McGregor's work on Theory X and Theory Y managers,[6] and Herzberg's motivators and hygiene factors.[7] One way to sort out these different approaches to the study of motivation is to divide them into content theories (which focus on what motivates people, what energizes their behavior) and process theories (which stress how motivation occurs in the surrounding environment). Here are some better-known motivation theories.

Well-Known Motivation Theories

Proponent	Theory	Key Concepts
Content Focus:		
Maslow	Hierarchy of needs (from low to high): Survival Security Social Self-esteem Self-actualization	Everyone has same set of five needs but in different degrees and at different times; lower needs must be met before higher ones can be activated.
Herzberg	Two-factor theory: Motivators (like achievement, responsibility, advancement, challenge, growth) and hygiene factors (like organizational policies, pay, benefits, supervision, and working conditions)	Hygiene factors keep people on the job; motivators produce superior performance.
McClelland et al.	High achievement needs	People with high achievement needs like to set their own goals, making them moderately high; they need immediate, frequent, and measurable feedback.[8]
Process Focus:		
Vroom	Expectancy theory	Peoples' motivation depends on extent to which they expect to receive those things that are important to them for excellent behavior.[9]

Proponent	Theory	Key Concepts
Skinner	Operant conditioning	Focus on behavior to be changed; reward "good" behavior, ignore "bad"; use rewards that person values; link rewards to appropriate behavior as close in time as possible.[10]

Maslow prescribed participative decision making; Herzberg advocated job enrichment; McClelland called for management by objectives. With such a variety of approaches and prescriptions to increase motivation, the picture becomes even more fuzzy. It soon becomes obvious that library managers must look not only at the broad spectrum of needs and motivation but also at significant individual differences. They must assess need satisfaction among their staff but avoid the trap of assuming that measures of job satisfaction relate directly to motivation or job effectiveness. Improvements in job satisfaction do not necessarily cause improvements in productivity.

To Persuade

We define persuasion as the attempt by one person or group of people to modify the behavior of another person or group. Although all communication is, in a sense, persuasive (if nothing else, we want people to listen to us or read what we have written), the usual goal of persuasion is to influence some one to change his/her way of thinking and/or acting.

The most effective persuaders focus on satisfying their persuadees' needs. Salespeople, for example, stress the benefits of their products and help customers visualize themselves enjoying those benefits. Similarly, advertisers of new products start by trying to convince potential customers that they have needs they didn't know they had; they then offer a product that will magically meet those newly found needs.

Effective managers know that ideas need to be sold, not just told, and that persuasion is necessary for people to arrive at common goals and harmonize work efforts. Yet persuasion is an elusive phenomenon, partly because it is difficult to measure people's attitudes, and partly because expressed attitudes may not reflect actual behavior. What people do is probably of greater importance to us than what people say they do or what they say they should do.

Although these and other variables complicate our view of "truths" about persuasion, communication researchers have established the following givens.

- New information is more likely to have effect when the persuadee knows little about the subject.
- The more important or central an issue is to a person, the more resistant s/he will be to persuasive attempts.
- The more entrenched are the persuadee's feelings about the subject, the less likely s/he will change opinion.
- The farther away the persuader is from the persuadee in time and distance, the less effect the persuasion will have.
- Belief is passive, but doubt is active.

Persuaders use a variety of methods, each with direct implications for communication, to achieve the change they are after. Perhaps the oldest known is the use of authority, in which an expert opinion is used to bolster the persuader's prestige or credibility. Facts and figures and hard- headed "logic" are often tried as means of persuasion, but they are seldom successful all by themselves. (If logic alone persuaded, no one would still be smoking cigarettes.)

Another persuasive technique is that of association—linking two ideas together. Generally, one idea is already well-accepted, while the second may be novel; if you agree with the first, then surely you must agree with the second. For example, if one work unit is using a new procedure successfully and with good results, a supervisor might inquire why successful use is not possible in another area.

Persuaders know that people prefer a state of balance or equilibrium. If a staff member turns in shoddy work or if the boss suddenly shouts angrily at us, our feeling of equilibrium is lost and we are in a state of tension. Persuaders may try to deliberately create this sense of imbalance. People then respond by ignoring the message, rejecting the information, devaluing the new information, or rejecting the old attitude and accepting the new one. If a credible persuader has communicated a clear message that is personalized to us, we probably won't choose to ignore, reject, or devalue the information. The result is successful persuasion.

Paul Timm suggests that persuaders consider the scope (the difficulty in complying with the message's request) and cost (the trade-off required) for the person or group being persuaded.[11] Scope and cost can be psychological, or they can refer to physical or tangible resistance to change. An example of this would be a department head asking for a 20-percent budget increase, knowing the university is in financial difficulties and literally can't afford to give more. Another barrier in this same situation is that the dean has gone on record against any budget increases; to him/her, backing down would raise a pride issue. The successful persuader looks at scope and cost from the persuadee's point of view in order to tell how much persuasive effort will be needed.

To Instruct and/or Train

From new employee orientation to reassigned job responsibilities to major library changes, each librarian continually learns. Consequently, instruction and training comprise an important and ongoing process. Instructing and being instructed occur at all levels and in all positions. Instructional messages give "how to" information designed to enable employees to do their jobs the way they need to be done. These messages couple information with standards and requirements that determine how tasks are to be accomplished.

The difference between informing and instructing is vast. Although a supervisor can tell a new reference librarian that several recent interviews with patrons were not satisfactory and can even explain why they were unsatisfactory, instructing the reference librarian in how to do better interviews requires more than information.

Communication cannot be instructional unless it is clear. It must be direct, specific, to the point, and relatively free of external distraction. Often, on-the-job instruction is provided by those who held the job previously or by peers or supervisors. It can be a formal process with an overall sequence and explanation followed by specific, step-by-step procedures, many of which are demonstrated by the instructor, then practiced by the learner. Or it can be an infrequent question about policy or procedure answered by a colleague or an official manual.

Sources of instruction can range from a safety poster to a colleague at a nearby desk. The intent of instruction can be to broaden awareness, to deepen background knowledge, to upgrade existing performance, or to build new skills. When presented on a one-to-one basis, successful instruction depends heavily on interpersonal communication skills. With group instruction, the instructor must obviously understand and make use of group communication skills and forces.

Methods for instruction and training vary. Simulations, case studies, films, or videotapes, role playing—all differ in their ability to connect the individual with the instructional message. Their effectiveness varies, depending on clarity and quality of the method along with the acceptance of the learner and his/her preferred learning style.

Again, two-way communication is essential. Instruction and training should be evaluated to determine if they were effective. Did the learner learn? Was the desired outcome achieved? Was the behavior change long-lasting or in need of reinforcement later on? This process requires a base of trust, and an interactive process for eliciting feedback about the effectiveness of the training as well as the performance of the learner.

Work relationships built on the basis of on-the-job instruction often can strengthen the ability of the library's staff to work as a team because lines of communication have been opened and connections established that can be adapted for other types of work communication when needed.

To Coach and/or Discipline

In some cases, managers and supervisors must go beyond the usual on-the-job training to work with employees to enable them to perform at higher levels. Coaching is a process of analyzing the ways in which a mediocre or unsatisfactory job is being performed and working with the employee to get him/her to change and grow. Skillful coaching is an important form of preventive discipline.

When a manager spots unsatisfactory performance, the first step in the coaching process is to find out what is influencing the unsatisfactory performance (perhaps there are factors beyond the employee's control), whether the employee knows his/her performance isn't what it should be, and whether the employee knows the difference between his/her performance and a satisfactory one. Face-to-face confidential discussion between the employee and the supervisor should deal with specific behaviors of the employee. Statements such as "Your attitude needs improvement" or "Your interpersonal skills aren't good enough" give vague rather than specific feedback. More direct, clear, and helpful messages would be "Jane, your last three reports were not turned in on time" or "John, you made three cataloging errors yesterday."

Fournies points out that a vital ingredient in the coaching process is to get agreement from the employee that a problem exists.[12] The employee may not feel there is a problem or that it is his/her problem. As an example, suppose the library director places a high value on promptness and is distressed when Mary is consistently late. The director may frown at Mary or look at his/her watch, assuming that this nonverbal message is enough to convey that Mary's behavior needs correcting. However, Mary may not place a high value on promptness, feeling that her taking a shortened lunch period and frequently working overtime more than compensate for occasionally being a few minutes late in the morning. The director will probably have a hard time coaching Mary to change her behavior because of the assumption that Mary understands the problem and agrees that a problem exists.

The goal of coaching, in addition to improving employee performance, could be job enrichment or even preparation for future job assignments. Coaching is usually conducted privately, in a one-on-one format, and informally, with detailed discussions of issues and viewpoints as well as specific feedback and planning. Its communication style is more akin to tutoring than to instruction.

Ideally, coaching precedes disciplinary action, but coaching is not always the answer to personnel problems. Discipline may be needed in those rare instances when coaching fails or when the employee chooses not to change behavior. For discipline to bring about the desired change, consequences in response to poor performance must be clear and prompt. Ultimate consequences may take the form of a written (documented) reprimand in the person's file, demotion, or dismissal. In view of the seriousness of discipline, good interpersonal communication as well as conflict management skills are often required.

To Counsel

Counseling staff members is important for employees at all levels who struggle with personal problems that affect work performance. Old-style managers used to believe that personal problems should be left at home and never be brought to work. Today, we know that this is impossible; our personal lives and our world of work intertwine.

The colleague or staff member who serves as counselor for a fellow employee needs, first of all, to be a skilled listener. The effective counselor also needs to listen nonjudgmentally and refrain from giving advice or suggestions. Usually, the person in need of counseling only wants someone to listen, ask clarifying questions, and give objective feedback. Often, a troubled person will be able to solve his/her own problems with the aid of an empathetic counselor.

Those who counsel fellow employees must be on guard to avoid getting into areas for which they are not qualified. On-the-job counseling is not psychotherapy; if more than a sympathetic ear is required, the would-be counselor should recommend a more qualified person within the organization or a professional therapist.

To Mentor

Mentoring, like coaching and counseling, is an interpersonal exchange requiring one-to-one communication skills. Mentors are keys to personal development and growth, to career advancement, and to valuable guidance and information. Usually, a mentor and protégé find each other, for the relationship must be based on mutual trust and respect. Some relationships evolve naturally from shared interests, proximity, and need; others are deliberately sought by either mentor or protégé; still others are designated by the organization whereby new employees are assigned a mentor in an officially sanctioned "buddy system."

Mentors are often older, more experienced people who know organizational policies, politics, and pitfalls and are willing to share their knowledge with newer employees. Protégés, usually new or inexperienced people, need this information and advice. The mentor's messages offer both explicit guidance and implicit help through the mentor's modeling what is appropriate behavior for success and advancement in that particular organization. A protégé can seek out a mentor for information about the library that does not appear on the organizational chart. Insider information is personally tailored to fit with the protégé's interests and goals, thus, mentors serve as allies for career development. With such a personal approach, communication must be open and trusting, objective, and frank as well as helpful.

To Develop Staff

Obviously, prepared, skilled staff are essential in the library. On-the-job instruction, coaching, counseling, and mentoring all contribute to employee effectiveness. In addition, training opportunities outside of the library, at conferences and workshops for example, return in-depth skills and new ideas to the library. Remember, though, that making such opportunities available to the staff does not ensure that growth and development will happen automatically.

Staff development requires planning and a coordinated program. Most sizeable libraries use various methods to guide employee growth and integrate them with organizational development. In addition to learning opportunities, other methods include incentives for improved performance such as merit pay, public affirmation, promotion, and praise, as well as structures that promote and enable upward mobility and job enrichment.

Staff development is an area, not unlike the others described here, that is very sensitive to the need for good communication. A major reason is that everyone involved has much at stake. Individual employees' careers and work satisfaction are affected. Managers are dealing with the most complex and costly of library resources and with the success of their assigned responsibilities. Such stakes involve emotions and make effective communication particularly significant and additionally difficult.[13]

Formal performance appraisal systems are staff development programs that are intended to ensure high productivity and guide employee growth. The prescribed process—written evaluation forms and regular discussions between supervisor and employee—when used properly, institutionalize communication lines. They are designed to ensure that perspectives, requirements, standards, and limitations are discussed by employees with their supervisors. Given clear and honest communication without just going through the motions, such systems can work very well.

Appraisal forms usually use rating terms like "excellent" and "average." These are only rubber yardsticks unless those involved discuss and share their meanings for the criteria used to arrive at the ratings. A technique used less often, but even more valuable, is the practice of blending employee goal setting with organizational goals. Higher productivity and morale are inevitable results when such internal communication systems are geared to help individual staff members learn and grow.

Staff members also develop and grow as a result of the supervisory and management styles utilized in the library. These, together with the personalities of supervisors and managers, create the climate of the library. A climate where information is shared through clear and functioning communication channels results in a healthy organization which fosters personal and career development.

Such a climate is not created simply by declaring it exists. Good communication as an organizational value and a standard of behavior is an important first step to create that kind of climate. Even so, a supportive climate requires nurturing over time, nurturing that results from supervisors and staff listening to and respecting each other. Open discussion of issues, changes, and capabilities keep all levels informed so they can perform appropriately on the job and so they can develop themselves and the library. (Climate is discussed in greater detail in Chapter 3, "Special Concerns of Library Managers.")

To Build Teams

In the press of daily activities, organizations sometimes neglect the building of esprit de corps; tasks are done but at the expense of organizational health. This can happen when too much emphasis in the organization is placed on developing individual skills and not enough is put on developing the ability of people to work together. The team concept can have a dramatic, positive impact on productivity and enthusiasm because a cohesive, highly motivated team can consistently outperform a collection of talented individuals.

One benefit of team building is the exploration of human diversity—the differences that individuals have in values, approach, and style. Such differences can build walls between people and hinder progress and projects. But teams can learn to value and capitalize on diversity once they see it as a strength and a source for even greater momentum.

Organizations have many types of teams: the departmental or work group "family" team, equal rank or status team, technical or functional team, special project or task force team, planning or problem-solving team, and top management team. Teams work effectively if they have common goals, a basic mission, and if they carefully coordinate their activities.

Choosing the Most Effective Media for Internal Communication

Media, as we use the term here, refers to specific methods selected to transmit messages. In broad terms, internal communication can be transmitted through words, pictures, symbols, or actions. More specifically, we must decide whether to use the telephone or call a meeting. Each of us usually develops our favorite method for transmitting principal internal messages. Some are "memo happy"; others rely heavily on one-to-one oral exchanges. Certain media may get to be favorites, unfortunately, not because of their favorable impact on listeners or readers but because of habit or tradition or because they are quick and easy media for the manager to use.

People seldom notice or think about the medium through which a message arrives. When they receive a good letter, they are more conscious of the message than the medium. The receiver may not know or care that the sender had to make many decisions even before writing the letter: to whom it would go, which medium would work best for the purpose and whether to send a single message through a single medium or to use a combination of methods if the message is complex.

Sometimes multiple media are best because using more than one method can ensure that an important message will get through; an example would be using both a newsletter and notices on bulletin boards to remind employees of an important staff meeting. On the other hand, sometimes a single medium will do the job; more might only produce irritation from information overload. For example, too many reminders may gall responsible people who keep their calendars up-to-date and faithfully attend announced meetings.

Choosing from among available media is best done with the following factors in mind: the complexity of the message, its importance to the sender and receiver, the urgency and cost of delay, the desired response or purpose, and the number and location of the message's receivers. Sometimes a written memo is a wise choice—as when the message is not urgent and no response is required. Sometimes holding a meeting is unwise, as when people routinely report what is going on in their units and there are no decisions to make or problems to solve. "Show-and-tell" information could be better handled through written reports, with a great savings of staff time. If, on the other hand, a department head calls a staff meeting to do some team building or clear the air on an issue causing conflict, written reports would never accomplish the same results as a meeting with face-to-face interaction.

How can we tell which media work best for a given message and purpose we may have in mind? The following chart analyzes the principal media used for internal communication. Note that some of the media apply to library users as well as to staff.

Internal Media Analysis

Media	Strengths	Weaknesses	Comments
Announcements, instructions	Useful for presenting general information about the library, its policies and procedures. Available in permanent form. Useful to back up orientation and training.	May not be generalizable to more than one group of staff. Managers may not want some policies made public. Over time, mass of instructions may add up to red tape, reducing manager's initiative.	Most suitable for important messages affecting entire organization or of interest to large numbers of people.
Attitude and opinion surveys (staff & users)	Offer a means of learning what staff and users think and want. Include implicit message that management wants to know. Can cover many areas, subjects.	Polls difficult to design, administer, analyze. May not get honest, objective information. Small return may not represent true cross section.	Respondents usually strongly biased for or against.
Brochures, pamphlets, flyers	Suitable for a variety of subjects. Convenient to distribute. May be used as "stuffer" or displayed.	Require time, skill for writing, layout, artwork. "Throw away" attribute may make them expensive.	Most effective when professionally produced and used as supplement to other media.
Bulletin boards, chalkboards	Convenient, inexpensive, highly flexible. Easily changed. Well-suited for brief, timely news.	Limited space. Cannot be effectively targeted. Require regular clearing. Not useful for long messages.	Eye appeal, clear incentives, and strategic placement essential.

Internal Media Analysis (continued)

Media	Strengths	Weaknesses	Comments
Cassette tapes	Useful for library news or instruction.	Staff may resent using personal time to listen to work-related topics. Equipment required.	Useful for staff who commute by car.
Displays, exhibits, information racks	Can quickly tell a story, introduce new material, or explain a service. Useful way to display casual, changing material on broad subjects and make items available to be picked up. High attention value.	Reading and selection of material voluntary; no control over who reads or takes material. Erecting, servicing, dismantling required.	Eye appeal and strategic placement essential.
Interviews	Good source for giving and getting information in private setting.	Time-consuming. Require skill to conduct.	Patterned questions work best if more than one person is to be asked about the same subject.
Manuals, handbooks	Codify instructions, save time and trouble. Explain tested procedures. Provide constant reference. Useful for orientation.	Difficult, time-consuming, costly to prepare. Need constant updating. Difficult to keep current and readable.	Commonly used medium to inform and train, especially new staff.

Internal Media Analysis (continued)

Media	Strengths	Weaknesses	Comments
Meetings	Useful for problem solving and decision making when exchange of ideas and opinions is valuable. Provide immediate feedback. Also aid in team building.	Can waste time if group allowed to stray off agenda. Can be expensive in terms of lost staff time.	Purpose of meeting should be clear. Some groups meet out of habit rather than need.
Memos, bulletins	Flexible, quickly produced and distributed. Provide documentation, permanent record, and act as reminders. Convey or request information. Establish or confirm policy, authority. Can be formal or informal, personalized or targeted generally.	Tend to be "dashed off" and overworked. Require filing. Unless carefully tracked, can reflect inconsistencies and contradictions in policy.	Backbone of documentation process. Work best if limited to a single point or theme.
Newsletters, house organs	Present organizational positions, policies in newsy, informal format. Can reach many readers quickly. Flexible, convenient, inexpensive, and can be somewhat personalized. Can also serve ombudsperson function.	Require reporting and writing skill, as well as adequate budget to make attractive. May be conflict between library news and personal or gossip features.	Depending on skill of staff, such publications can be effective means of communicating important "inside" messages.

Internal Media Analysis (continued)

Media	Strengths	Weaknesses	Comments
Policy statements, procedural rules	Clarify organization mission, specific procedures, such as purchasing, accounting. Provide reference, especially for new staff.	Difficult to initiate, amend, or get approved. Compilation and organization require skill, effort, filing methods. Sometimes difficult to distinguish between ordinary memo and policy announcement.	Useful if well-organized, regularly updated, made conveniently available. Work best when explaining what should *not* be done.
Posters, signs	Attention-getting. Easy to understand. Useful for announcements and occasional reminders.	Limited to single, simple themes. Require some artistic skill and regular replacement.	Eye appeal and strategic placement essential. Effective as part of information campaign.
Preprinted forms	Blank spaces for fill-ins save words, time. Useful shortcuts for regular reporting of repetitive activities. Ensure standardization of information presentation.	Tend to be dull, regimented. Can't be personalized. May discourage initiative, be viewed as "red tape."	Can expedite procedures like accounting. Complex forms require instructions or training.
Reports	Provide in-depth information, problem identification, solution, and permanent record. Evaluate progress, efficiency. Useful for decision making.	Require skills of analysis, organization, writing. Take time, effort. Tend to be too long, involved; encourage scanning rather than reading.	Essential to management control.

Internal Media Analysis (continued)

Media	Strengths	Weaknesses	Comments
Special events	Can be planned for specific purpose, such as honoring staff or volunteers. Cause only short-term interruption of work flow.	Require staff time to plan, promote, and administer.	Good morale boosters.
Suggestion systems (staff)	Provide opportunities for upward communication, ways to improve policies, procedures. Encourage creativity, high morale. Can vary from suggestion box to columns in newsletter.	Sometimes difficult to convince staff that suggestions are sincerely wanted and will be acted upon. Planning, methods, and personnel required. Need constant promotion, reminders, and follow-up.	Best administered by committee. Work best when rewards are given for greater efficiency or improved service or functioning.
(users)	When user complaints or suggestions are communicated directly to the staff or unit involved, the work becomes more important and the relationship between the work and user satisfaction better understood. Clarifies unit or library standards.	Require methods, forms, personnel. Difficult to solicit on regular basis and present in coherent, organized way. Difficult to distinguish between one dissatisfied user and public at large.	A good way to involve users and assess attitudes about service.

Internal Media Analysis (continued)

Media	Strengths	Weaknesses	Comments
Telephone	Fast, direct. Allows immediate feedback. Conference calls less expensive than bringing people in from other units, branches.	Because of convenience, often overworked when other media would perform better. Unless recorded, or notes taken, leaves no documentation.	Most important internal communication linking system. Works best if all important decisions are followed up by written confirmation.
Videotape	Closed circuit TV is fine tool for training, evaluating service and performance, and recording key meetings. Lightweight portable models have high flexibility.	Cost/benefit ratio must be considered. Technical training needed for maximum benefit.	A closed circuit transmission system with multiple monitors could be of benefit to larger libraries or library systems. Top management can communicate with small groups of staff.

Summary of Internal Media

Message forms and formats themselves become messages. How you choose to communicate may carry more weight than the ideas conveyed or the words themselves. Media can indirectly (but powerfully) influence policy. An established, long-standing policy manual, for example, may cause people to tailor new policies to fit *the manual,* rejecting new policies that might require extensive manual revision.

The effective selection of media deserves more attention than it usually gets. The appearance (handwritten or typed), quality of transmission, and timing of your communication may either enhance or counteract the effort you have put into its content and organization. Your selection can improve based on your understanding of each medium's strengths and weaknesses and their basic criteria. Each medium choice can be a message in itself.

EXTERNAL COMMUNICATION

In contrast to internal communication, external communication consists of messages the library exchanges with outside elements. As with internal communication, these messages and the channels through which they flow are intended to convey information that the library wants the audience to know and that the audience needs to know. These messages must be carefully crafted to get the right information to the right people.

An external message might be a publicity release to the local newspaper about a new acquisition or branch; it might be telephone contacts to key civic groups and businesses to promote a new service. Unintentional messages are delivered by the appearance of the building and grounds, staff courtesy and service, or a "flap" reported in the newspaper about an incident involving collecting overdue fines.

A library has many publics with which to communicate. Although circumstances vary with individual libraries, a typical list of groups with which the library needs to maintain contact would include the following.

- Library users and potential users.
- The community, campus, company, or school at large.
- Other units of the library's organization (such as public library branches or school administration for the school library).
- Other libraries.
- Library networks.
- Charitable groups and individual donors.
- Government bodies (such as city councils and school boards).
- Civic groups (such as the Chamber of Commerce).
- Educational institutions.
- Professional associations.
- Staff associations and unions.
- Consultants.
- Providers of service and supplies (vendors).

Each organization in these categories is composed of individual personalities, and each has an organizational structure. Consequently, communication between and among organizations becomes exceedingly complex. But just as you have become adept at communicating with various personalities in your work, so you can also become skilled at being a representative of one organization (the library) communicating with other organizations' representatives. According to Dance:

> Good public service is the foundation for good PR (public relations). There are various aspects of building and improving public service; here we shall mention only one: The importance of 'consciousness raising' on the part of the entire staff, however

small, however large. If you can get your staff members to recognize the PR impact of each function they perform and each contact they make, you will have laid the groundwork for much future success.[14]

Clear, effective external messages require clear, effective internal communication. The right kind and amount of information as well as its timeliness are even more vital since often a receiver may get only one message and s/he cannot be tracked to correct misinformation. Two-way communication can help ensure that the appropriate information is reaching the right people.

But many elements, such as timing and channel may be beyond the individual communicator's control. Understanding the nature of organizational communication will increase your awareness of the many factors at work. With this awareness, you can discover the formal and informal routes to get information into and from another organization.

As with internal communication, each external communication involves purpose, channel, and media choices. The typical purposes for external communication follow.

- To communicate: establish and maintain effective, open, two-way communication channels between library personnel and the groups listed above.
- To become visible: project an image to the public of what the library is like and what services it offers.
- To promote: attract new users rather than passively waiting for new users to appear.
- To provide leadership: serve as a positive influence in the community and to make the library a focal point for community concerns, activities, and support.
- To create connections: ensure that the library is in touch with other libraries, library associations, and allied professional organizations for mutual problem solving and to keep up with developments in the field.
- To negotiate: work with library boards and governmental (or institutional) organizations in order to maintain or improve the library's financial and other support.

The choice of effective media for external communication should be carefully considered. It is all too easy to fall into a rut and continually use the same pattern. With the aid of the following chart, which analyzes the principal media used for external communication, librarians can expand their repertoires of ways to communicate with individuals and groups outside of the organization.

External Media Analysis

Media	Strengths	Weaknesses	Comments
Advertise-ments	Newspaper and magazine insertions are convenient, reach wide audience for relatively low cost. Electronic media are more expensive for production and time but worth considering. Useful for announcements, gaining support, or to take stand on public issues.	Difficult to gauge impact unless "free offer" or some follow-up means planned. Electronic message highly perishable; amount of prime time limited.	Should supplement rather than replace other media.
Articles, news releases, reprints	Build, maintain prestige via trade journals, association presses, as well as local newspapers. New services, special events can be announced at little cost; reprints can be shared later with wider audience.	Require news slant, careful planning, preparation. Best written by professionals. May have long lag time before publication so not effective for timely or urgent messages.	Cannot guarantee material will be published or read.
Billboards, posters	Allow repetition of message; low cost; geographic selectivity; in view 24 hours a day.	Message must be short and simple. Seldom get full attention.	May be criticized as unaesthetic.

External Media Analysis (continued)

Media	Strengths	Weaknesses	Comments
Brochures, pamphlets, flyers, tote bags	Flexibility of subjects. Convenient to distribute. May be mailed or used as "stuffers."	Require skill in writing, layout, artwork. Because of "throwaway" attribute, may be expensive in terms of short life.	Most effective when professionally produced and used as supplement to other media.
Form letters, direct mail pieces	Flexible; can reach many people with same message quickly. Less expensive than individual letters.	Require printing and staff time for mailing list maintenance, "stuffing," and stamping.	"Canned" message may have negative impact if trying to masquerade as personal letter.
Meetings of outside groups	Library staff, as members or guests of influential community organizations, can effectively communicate about the library.	Staff need skill and sensitivity in knowing what and when to communicate.	It is sometimes difficult to get the right people invited to join targeted groups.
Personal letters	Familiar medium that can be both informative and provide documentation. Can go to one person or several. Easy to produce and to reach people at a distance. High impact if personalized.	May encourage time lag if response is slow in coming. Require filing.	Universally accepted and widely used medium. Electronic mail will speed up process.

External Media Analysis (continued)

Media	Strengths	Weaknesses	Comments
Public presenta-tions	Whether done on an individual basis or as part of speakers' bureau, is quick, dynamic method of dispensing information, particularly if feedback and questions are encouraged.	Require skill, effective audiovisual aids, and time for both preparation and presentation.	Many clubs and associations continually look for program material.
Public service announce-ments	Free print space and air time may be available for special use.	Material must fit media guidelines.	Often overlooked opportunity.
Special events	Can be planned for specific purpose such as attracting new users, showing off new equipment, or honoring staff or volunteers. Cause only short-term interruption of work flow and service.	No guarantee of hoped-for attendance. Require staff time for planning, promoting, administering, and cleanup afterward.	If well-publicized, a good way to keep the library in the public eye.
Telephone	Fast, direct. Allows immediate feedback. Good medium for informing, persuading.	Because of convenience, often overworked when other media would perform better.	Works best if all important decisions are followed up by written confirmation.

Creative choice and use of fresh media to present the library's message can help reach new people, change the library's image, and enhance its public relations. Telling the library's story by telephone and personal letters is a good personal approach. But this one-by-one method is slow, time-consuming, and costly. Brochures and public service announcements are more commonly used now and reach a wider (and different) audience. Each situation offers new opportunities that should be seized.

Knowing each medium's strengths and weaknesses enables library personnel to make wiser choices. And, of course, constant evaluation of external communication results will ensure that choices are based on effectiveness, not on whim or guesswork.

NOTES

1. Morton F. Meltzer, *The Information Imperative* (New York: American Management Association, 1971), pp. 94–95.

2. Meltzer, p. 91.

3. John R. Rizzo, *Management for Librarians* (Westport, CT: Greenwood Press, 1980), p. 133.

4. A. H. Maslow, *Motivation and Personality* (New York: Harper, 1954, 1970).

5. E. A. Locke, "Toward a Theory of Task Motivation and Incentives," *Organizational Behavior and Human Performance* 3 (2) (May 1968): pp. 157–89.

6. Douglas McGregor, *The Human Side of Enterprise* (New York: McGraw-Hill, 1960) and *The Professional Manager* (New York: McGraw-Hill, 1967).

7. Frederick Herzberg, *Work and the Nature of Man* (Cleveland, OH: World Publishing, 1966).

8. David C. McClelland et al., *The Achievement Motive* (New York: Appleton-Century- Crofts, 1953) and *The Achieving Society* (Princeton, NJ: D. Van Nostrand Co., Inc., 1961).

9. Victor H. Vroom, *Work and Motivation* (New York: John Wiley and Sons, 1964).

10. B. F. Skinner, *Beyond Freedom and Dignity* (New York: Alfred A. Knopf, 1971).

11. Paul R. Timm, *Functional Business Presentations* (Englewood Cliffs, NJ: Prentice-Hall, Inc., 1981).

12. Ferdinand F. Fournies, *Coaching for Improved Work Performance* (New York: Van Nostrand Reinhold Company, 1978).

13. Barbara Conroy, *Library Staff Development and Continuing Education* (Littleton, CO: Libraries Unlimited, Inc., 1978), p. 224.

14. James C. Dance, "Public Relations for the Smaller Library," *Small Libraries Publication, No. 4* (Chicago: Library Administration and Management Association, American Library Association, 1979), p. 1.

Chapter 3
Special Concerns of Library
Managers

In line with this book's premise that libraries need a managed organizational communication system, this chapter begins with that as the most important managerial concern, goes on to show how such a system can be developed and evaluated, and then discusses some specific leadership and organizational concerns.

MANAGING ORGANIZATIONAL COMMUNICATION

Organizational communication is (or should be) the concern of everyone. Yet the ultimate responsibility for initiating and evaluating the library's communication system must obviously rest with the top management. Along with those duties typically ascribed to managers, such as planning, organizing, integrating, and measuring, must surely be added that of managing communication.

Klauss and Bass are not content to have communication merely listed as one of several managerial functions. They write:

> ". . . managerial communication is probably one of the most critical areas of organizational communication in general and . . . it is the point at which managerial behavior can genuinely make a difference in influencing performance and employee attitudes. And if we consider the amount of time spent on communication on the part of managers, clearly its centrality to the manager's overall job cannot be denied."[1]

Of course, no one style of communication works for all library managers. Not only are personal variables such as knowledge, education, and values significant, but institutional variables such as size and mission have an impact. All of these affect how a manager communicates. What's more, within each manager is a repertoire of communication styles to fit varying circumstances and contingencies.

Communication is central to the manager's role because all of the manager's functions are accomplished through oral and written communication. Even if the duties are lumped under broad categories like "coordinate" or "select priorities," it is difficult to imagine five minutes of a manager's day that does not involve communication.

A key factor in successful organizational communication is the manager's attitude about what communication is and how it works. If the manager respects the value of managed communication and the individual staff member's right to information, that attitude is communicated by behavior as well as words. This attitude provides a model for effectively dealing with communication, and a standard to follow.

Library managers have a responsibility to find out where their staff members go for information. In a survey of over 45,000 employees in the United States and Canada, Selma Friedman found that the number one current source, as well as preferred source, was the employee's supervisor; yet 90.3 percent of those surveyed said they would like to be getting more information from their managers than they actually got. The second highest ranking source, according to the survey, was the grapevine, while the third source was employee booklets. Friedman also asked what information employees most wanted and found that they wanted to know about (in rank order) their organization's future plans, personnel policies and practices, productivity improvement, and job-related information.[2]

Another factor is the manager's objectivity in dealing with messages. Is the manager capable of accepting, assimilating, and acting on information that conflicts with his/her personal values and stereotypes? Is the manager able to detect information (from memos to formal reports) that is incomplete, distorted, or, at best, slanted?

As he departed, a retiring library director said to his successor (the former assistant director), "Yesterday was the last day you heard the truth from your subordinates." This may be an exaggeration, but it points to the real and persistent problem of getting accurate and complete upward communication.

Of course, managerial style influences how a manager communicates and provides personal criteria by which s/he will evaluate how others communicate. For example, a bureaucratic manager, whose main focus is in following the rules and going through the right channels, will also expect (and even require) that behavior from others. This may result in the library getting bogged down in details, losing sight of the mission that the communication is intended to further. In contrast, a manager valuing participative involvement will disseminate information broadly and expect the same from others.

CRITERIA FOR AN EFFECTIVE COMMUNICATION SYSTEM

A communication program obviously needs to be well-planned, systematic, and continuous. What's more, every managerial action must include planning for communication.

As managers develop and evaluate their own library communication systems, they will obviously build in adaptations for their unique situations, as well as for the inevitable crises and contingencies. The following is recommended only as a beginning checklist either to help you get started or to evaluate a communication system already in place.

What Should Be Communicated

People should be told those things that: (1) make them feel they belong, that they are "in on things," and that their work makes a difference; (2) demonstrate there is both opportunity and security in the organization; (3) reduce confusion, anxiety, and indifference; and (4) they will eventually learn for themselves.

Who Should Be Informed

The major criterion for deciding who should receive information should be who needs the information for the performance of his/her duties, in order to better understand the organization and its way of doing business, or for the positive rewards of being included. Although the manager must try to avoid communication overload, the danger in giving favored individuals exclusive information is that others who might need or could profit from the information will resent not receiving it.

Who Should Inform

Regular channels should be used as often as possible when communicating information. Where there is a choice of who should tell, select a person who is personally highly acceptable and credible and who has the reputation for communicating accurately, clearly, and interestingly. Everyone on any level who receives information to be passed on to someone else shares the responsibility for passing it on as quickly and as accurately as possible.

The Timing of Communication

The information should obviously reach the recipient in time to be of some value, not after the fact. Important reports have been delayed because necessary data did not arrive in time; meeting notices have appeared after the scheduled meeting date because the chairperson underestimated the time necessary to reproduce and distribute the announcement.

ASSESSING COMMUNICATION EFFECTIVENESS

Once the organizational communication system is in place, the manager needs a variety of ongoing methods for monitoring and evaluation. An overzealous manager might try to evaluate every sender, message, channel, receiver, and response. Although the thoroughness would be commendable, the process would be both exhausting and futile. Unfortunately, assessing an organization's communication in any way is seldom undertaken because it appears to be such a formidable task. Only when a misunderstanding or misinterpretation causes a crisis do most organizations raise questions like "What held up that new policy statement so long?" or "Why was that procedure memo inaccurate?"

Despite all the evidence that written statements don't get the job done, many managers still rely principally on memos, letters, manuals, and announcements. As a result, more questions are raised than answered, upward communication and individual initiative are discouraged, and people complain about not knowing what is going on. As one disgruntled employee put it, "What we need around here is less paper and more talk."

At a minimum, managers should spot-check the results of their own communication, following a paper trail and/or consulting with the staff member at the end of the communication chain to see what s/he understood about the content and intent of a given message. Even better would be an ongoing plan for regularly assessing communication patterns that develop among different people at different levels in the organization. Best yet, larger libraries and library systems should consider arranging for a communication audit conducted by outside communication professionals. (More about this in the next section.)

One successful method for assessing organizational communication is a tracking questionnaire given to specific staff members. At the top of the form is a block of data (such as a new or revised policy) about which the respondent is asked such questions as (1) What part or parts of this information did you know before receiving this questionnaire? (2) From where did you receive the information? (3) How did you receive the information? and (4) From whom did you receive the information? Data collected in this way can be assembled like a jigsaw puzzle to show how information is disseminated or blocked within the organization.

Another way to assess organizational communication effectiveness is as a part of general problem identification. One service organization, for example, held a general meeting to discuss the questions "How are we doing?" and "How can we do better?" Staff members were encouraged to brainstorm a list of "Aspects of the work I am dissatisfied with." Here is a segment of the list generated.

- Too few volunteers.
- Constant search for money.
- Not enough time to develop close relationships.
- Changing rules.
- Too much paperwork.
- Director does not discuss budget and let us know where we stand.
- Key people don't visit the sites often enough.

As you can see, the communication problems surfaced along with others. They did not have to be labeled as "communication" concerns for the director and staff to recognize that is what they were.

Another assessment approach is to circulate questionnaires or hold group discussions on questions such as: How effective are the communication lines between management and staff? Which person or group do you communicate with most frequently? Why? How promptly are you informed about changes in library procedures? How well does your supervisor pass along information from upper echelons? How frequently are you consulted when changes need to be made that affect your job? How effective is our performance appraisal system?

In his "Staff Communication Questionnaire," Richard Emery advocates questions like "How do you receive most information about the library and your job?" "What type of information do you receive most regularly?" "With whom do you have the most communication related to library matters and necessary for the performance of your duties?" "With whom do you have the most communication related to library matters but which is not necessary for the performance of your duties?"[3]

Another schema for assessing organizational communication is to identify your major managerial functions and then evaluate the effectiveness of the messages used both to perform these functions and to communicate about them. If the manager not only performs these functions but also pays attention to their communication components, assessment is built in. Added to the manager's assessment should be evaluations gathered from staff at all levels involved. Asking an employee how well a new policy was communicated may be the most direct way but probably, for reasons we have already pointed out, will not elicit what the manager really needs to know.

Evaluative feedback is the most difficult to get because it puts the employee's job in real or perceived jeopardy. Many methods have been tried to encourage honest responses, including providing forms (such as suggestion boxes and newsletter columns) for gripes and grievances, while at the same time protecting the employee's identity. Some organizations use an internal ombudsperson or an outside consultant to gather suggestions and/or problems from employees and then submit them to management in aggregate form. An electronics firm instituted a "Speak Up!" program in which employees could make anonymous written comments to the company newsletter editor and receive answers from management through the newsletter or a personal letter via the editor. A bank installed an "Open Line" program which offered a confidential means for any employee who wanted to submit a problem, complaint, or opinion to management. The writer, whose identity was known only to the Open Line Coordinator in the Communications Department, received a prompt written reply from management.

Assessments of organizational communication can vary from simply tallying the number of messages transmitted between people or units to a thorough evaluation of the quality of oral and written communication. In their "Self-Assessment Guide for Staff Communication," the Minnesota Office of Public Libraries and Interlibrary Cooperation lists different levels of competencies for employee-supervisor communication, peer communication, and language usage.[4] Such a guide not only helps the individual staff member to assess his/her own competencies but also provides resource lists and suggested ways the person can improve communication skills.

When research laboratory library staff in a large university discovered that information discussed at staff meetings was not being relayed to other personnel, they designed a unique solution. The newsletter editor now conducts informal, monthly interviews with each member of the professional staff and then compiles the information into comprehensive reporting of new developments and continuing projects.

COMMUNICATION AUDITS

Another means of evaluating organizational communication is the communication audit. Usually conducted by communication professionals, communication audits study messages as they flow within the organization. Goldhaber describes the audit process this way:

> "Just as an accountant audits the books of a large organization to determine its financial health, so does a communication consultant audit an organization's communicative climate to assess its health."[5]

Communication audits are commonly directed at such dimensions as the organization's philosophy regarding organizational communication, kinds of information exchanged, sources of information, quality of information, available channels and feedback, climate, relationships, and outcomes. From the data gathered and analyzed, consultants can provide management with an evaluation of the existing level of organizational communication effectiveness, point out current or potential trouble spots, and make recommendations for change or corrective action.

Small units or the entire organization can be audited. As with any system, stress in any part of the organizational communication will eventually make itself felt in other parts, perhaps far removed from the stress point itself. A communication audit can identify the cause of a communication breakdown even if it is in a different, less obvious part of the system than had been previously suspected.

Audit data are gathered through a variety of techniques, such as administering questionnaires, conducting interviews, making observations, performing network analyses, recording specific communicative events, evaluating samples of written material, and asking audit participants to keep track of their daily communication activities in an ongoing diary.

Some consultants not only record numbers of messages but also categorize them by their purpose and the function they serve. Some organizations prefer audits that evaluate individuals' communication effectiveness. Some formats call for individuals to rate themselves on criteria involving communication skills; the self-ratings are then compared with evaluations made by their subordinates, peers, and superiors. The goal of this kind of audit is to stimulate remedial efforts when a discrepancy is discovered between self-generated data and that provided by colleagues.

The audit developed by the International Communication Association (ICA) suggests the following as appropriate products of an audit:

1. An organizational profile based on perceptions of communication events, practices, and relationships.
2. A map of the operational communication network.
3. Explanations of the reasons for communication problems or strengths.
4. Individual communication profiles.
5. Some general recommendations for change.
6. Training of organizational personnel so that future audits can be conducted in-house.
7. Permanent (and confidential) future access to ICA audit bank so the organization can compare results with those of other organizations.[6]

In summary, a professionally conducted communication audit can be the means to system improvement. Obvious advantages exist for a professional rather than an amateurish approach, as well as for a comprehensive instead of a piecemeal diagnosis. Whether the audit is focused on internal communication between staff and departments or external communication with the library's publics, the specifics of what is to be audited and how the process will be handled must be carefully worked out in advance. Diagnoses of this type aren't so much "right" as they are useful. They provide a snapshot of how the organization's communication is working at the time. Since no communication program can be regarded as finished or permanently in place, evaluation should be continuous.

SPECIFIC PROGRAMS FOR MANAGING INFORMATION

As the result of a communication audit or other type of assessment of the communication in the organization, some managers decide they need a more formal system for managing information. Acquiring, organizing, and controlling information for effective decision making is the essence of management. It is clear today that information is a resource that must be managed for the same reasons that material and human resources need to be managed. Decisions that must be made on the basis of information can be visualized on a spectrum. At one end are routine operational decisions, based on simple information such as deciding to buy a duplicate title based on the first book's rate of use. At the other end of the spectrum are managerial decisions based on more ambiguous, complex, and diverse information, such as that for a performance appraisal.

Stevens points out that only a few libraries have developed methods to collect data systematically. He says, "Most libraries approach the collection and use of data on an ad hoc basis as the need arises and the situation demands."[7] As libraries become increasingly complex, with more specialized expertise and services to manage, however, many library administrators are developing or at least considering the adoption of what the business world calls a Management Information System (MIS). The MIS is a systematic set of strategies for collecting data, turning them into information, storing them until needed, then channeling the flow to decision makers, who use it to meet the needs of the organization. An MIS can be comprehensive or specific and used in automated or nonautomated libraries, large or small libraries, or in individual work units.

For an MIS to be effective, management must know what it wants and how to use the information. Collecting useless information (or information that won't be used effectively or at all) is, of course, utter waste. What's more, there is no point in using an elaborate method to collect information that is already known, or for which we have a simpler, more cost-effective method of gathering. Information resulting from the use of an MIS should enable managers to reduce costs, improve decision making, and/or lead to improvement in service.

Although large investments of time and resources may be required initially to change methods of data collection and recording, once the system is in place, it can provide information for management control, such as to design and implement plans and allocate resources. Perhaps the most useful function for an MIS, however, is its potential to integrate diverse activities through a common information pattern. According to Tague, the conception of a system like MIS preceded the computer, but the computer has made its full achievement possible; and automated subsystems can analyze operations in a way that overworked library staff have never been able to manage before.[8]

Growing out of MIS has been the Decision Support System (DSS), which has been described by Dowlin as a whole new direction or philosophy in computer-based management, rather than just a single invention or method.[9] Since DSS is intended to be an interactive process, allowing the manager to introduce variables, it can only be used in an automated library. The following chart, developed by McDonald,[10] contrasts MIS and DSS.

A Comparison of MIS and DSS

MIS	DSS
Passive use	Active use
Clerical activities	Line, staff, and management activities
Oriented toward mechanical efficiency	Oriented toward overall effectiveness
Focus on the past	Focus on the present and future
Emphasis on consistency	Emphasis on flexibility and ad hoc utilization

To understand how these two information systems fit into our concept of organizational communication, see Figure 10.

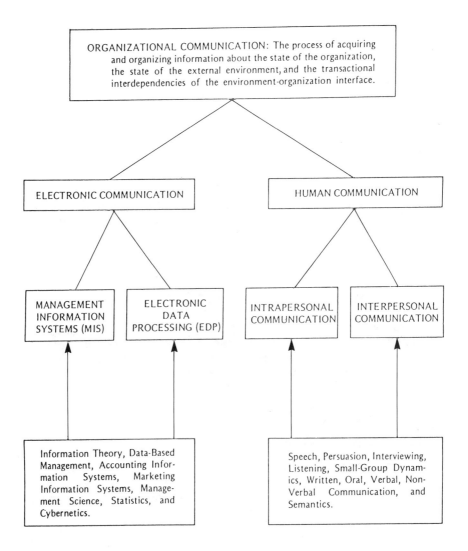

Figure 10. Organizational Communication: A Unified Framework.

Reprinted from "Organizational Communication: A Systems Viewpoint," by A. G. Kefalas, in Richard C. Huseman, Cal M. Logue, and Dwight L. Freshley, *Readings in Interpersonal and Organizational Communication*, 3rd ed., Boston: Allyn and Bacon, Inc., 1977, p. 41 (pp. 25–43).[11] Used by permission.

TYPICAL BARRIERS

An assessment of organizational communication may turn up one or more of the following fairly typical barriers:

Lack of Supportive Climate

People communicate better if they are working in a climate of confidence, mutual understanding, and a strong sense of common purpose. Does fear of rejection or disapproval restrict the flow of upward communication?

Lack of Motivation to Communicate

Managers need to model—and instill in others—the desire to communicate efficiently. Have people developed the habit of communicating only the minimum on the theory that the less they communicate, the fewer mistakes they can make or at least be charged with?

Lack of Feedback

People communicate, or believe that they do, and sit back, assuming that all is well. More careful attention to feedback might shatter this complacency and expose inadequacy. Managers need to know what is (and is not) getting through. The lack of feedback may give the message sender the false impression that his/her communication was not only received but also understood and approved.

Lack of Feedforward

In order to elicit feedback, people must take responsibility for sending clear and provocative preliminary messages that suggest direction and content of further communication. An explicit statement like "Today, I think we should discuss budget problems," points the way, whereas "Do you think we should discuss budget problems today?" serves as a trial balloon. Managers need to assess the quality of their initiating messages.

Failure to Understand or Tap the Grapevine

Managers who have suffered from problems caused by information leaks may be forgiven their wish to chop down the grapevine, that informal communication network that runs back and forth across organizational lines. Yet a lively grapevine reflects a healthy organization, one in which people talk about their jobs and their organization out of high interest and personal need. Far from being merely a rumor factory or gossip mill, the grapevine should be listened to by every manager. Research shows that even the wildest of stories making the rounds has a root cause and is at least partially true. Grapevine transmissions are at their highest in times of change or insecurity and particularly when there is a lack of substantive information emanating from management levels. Managers who do not accept and respect the grapevine, or who do not cultivate open channels of communication to offset it, may soon find themselves out of touch with what is really going on. Management's credibility is at stake if managers don't quickly come forward to correct or explain the full story behind the rumors. Merely denying a rumor is a waste of time.

LEADERSHIP CONCERNS

Because leadership is such a vast and complex subject, we obviously cannot include all possible ramifications. We have, therefore, selected those aspects that are most important to library managers.

To Lead or to Manage?

We often hear the complaint that there are lots of managers around but few leaders; that many institutions are well-managed but poorly led. (For example, people handle daily routines well but never question if those routines should be followed.) As with most clichés, there is some truth to the one that goes "Leaders do the right things, while managers do things right."

Better and more specific distinctions between leading and managing are these.

To lead = inspire commitment, show the way, influence, guide the group's direction and course of action
Keys: vision and judgment

To manage = bring about, accomplish, have responsibility for, conduct
Key: activities for efficiency

Leadership has little meaning except in relation to a task or goal, so getting the group's goals clarified and agreed to are important leadership functions. Another problem is the constant tension that comes from either a too-tight or a too-loose leadership rein. Groups often complain about a leader who is too controlling; yet most followers prefer a structured role so that they know what is expected of them.

Thanks to research and many publications on the subject, we know quite a bit about styles and functions of leadership. We know that leaders have a range of behaviors from strict authoritarian, to democratic, to laissez-faire upon which to draw. Most people are familiar with McGregor's Theory X and Theory Y, which were based on the leader's assumption that his/her subordinates were passive and resistant to organizational needs (Theory X) or that people already possess motivation and desire for responsibility (Theory Y).[12]

Since McGregor's well-known work, others have come out with Theory W and Theory Z and a variety of leadership styles and techniques. Examples are management by objectives (first labeled by Drucker[13]), which has become both a process and an overworked slogan; Fiedler's contingency model of leadership effectiveness, which attempted to integrate the effects of leadership styles and situational variables[14]; and Hersey and Blanchard's situational leadership styles, which are intended to demonstrate that there is no one best style for all situations[15].

Whether we think in terms of a leader's functions (what s/he actually does) or a leader's style (a consistent way of behaving), we recognize there are no simple descriptive labels that can be used. The question is not one of directive *or* permissive leadership. Instead, the question should be what kind of leadership is the most functional given the group's goals and stage of development? There is no standard management model or leadership style that works all of the time. No one knows for sure what makes good leadership in every situation. The best you can do is try to understand your organization and its requirements and then judge the extent to which your leadership contributes to or blocks progress—and the extent to which you are able to learn new skills if needed. The search for an effective, yet comfortable, style is personal and continuous.

In a survey of 90 leaders across the United States, 60 corporate executives and 30 from the public sector, Warren Bennis found they had four competencies in common:

1. Management of attention: the ability to keep people focused on a vision, goal, or direction.
2. Management of meaning: the ability to get people to understand and support the goals by integrating facts, concepts, and anecdotes into meaning.
3. Management of trust: the ability to establish reliability and constancy.

4. Management of self: the ability to know one's strengths and nurture them and keep them focused on the task, along with the ability to see setbacks as merely next steps, not failures.[16]

Clearly, all four competencies are dependent upon the leader's abilities to communicate.

Library directors need to be both leaders and managers. They need both a vision, which illuminates the difference between where their organizations are and where they could or should be, and the practical skills to effectively manage both day-to-day operations and consistent movement of the organization toward the vision. Communication is the tool to build and share the vision and to ensure operational follow through.

THE CASE FOR SHARED LEADERSHIP

The usual focus on a single leader in an organization is deeply rooted in the traditional system of patriarchal leadership. We are recognizing, however, that effective styles of leadership and management must be reflections of changing needs, forces, and circumstances. Different leadership structures are needed at different times in the development cycles of organizations. Attitudes about work relationships and employer-employee roles are undergoing change. Job enrichment, work modules, and self-governing employee teams such as "quality circles" all illustrate the evolving trends. Organizations and management consultants are collaborating to counteract some of the dehumanizing aspects of routine, assembly-line operations. They know that workers are happier when they can construct the job than when the job constructs them.

Despite the evidence to support the advantages of shared leadership, putting the concept into practice, particularly in large bureaucracies, seems to be as difficult as it has always been.

Perhaps one problem with getting more acceptance of the concept of shared leadership is the notion that it means worker control or "work place democracy" in which lower levels of employees take over from the top and start running the company. Rather than viewing shared leadership as giving up power, managers would do well to think in terms of empowerment of others and the sharing of power.

Leadership isn't a bag of tricks to get groups to act or to manipulate people. Leadership is a series of functions that all groups need; and almost all leaders are willing to admit there are too many functions to be performed well by only one person. With this in mind, it is clear that shared leadership is not a luxury but a necessity.

Real leadership develops, not dominates, individuals. There seems to be no substitute for the satisfaction people get from sharing decisions, responsibilities, and work. Although grooming others to take over more of the leader's functions might sound altruistic, it is, in reality, a hard-headed means of getting more work done and making the manager look good. So, sharing leadership is a practical method for achieving results. It turns out that two (or more) heads really are better than one.

THE SPECIAL PROBLEMS OF MIDDLE MANAGERS

Although top management and front line manager/supervisors have difficult positions to fill, middle managers seem to have the worst of both worlds; they are shot at from above and below. Since middle managers have one foot in each camp, they are not completely at ease or completely accepted in either.

Another problem those in the middle ranks face, especially if they are competent, dedicated workers, is having too much work assigned to them. This can result from overdelegation of authority by upper echelons. Decentralized authority has its advantages, but a potential negative is that by relinquishing authority, top management eventually knows less and less about what is going on. Overburdened middle managers, for example, may take time only to report what they feel is very important. As a result, other vital information could be buried.

Another problem is the glut of middle managers. In his book, *The Oppressed Middle: Politics of Middle Management,* Shorris makes the point that, as uncomfortable as the role of middle manager may be, there are growing numbers of them. He sees the baby boom generation causing a bulge in the ranks of middle managers because so few will be able to reach the top spots in the hierarchy. So add the element of fierce competition to the problems already experienced by those in the middle. Unfortunately, Shorris doesn't offer any easy answers.[17]

Although Oshry's answer isn't necessarily easy, he suggests that the challenge to middle staff is to be responsive to top and bottom staff, yet remain independent of them. He feels middle staff should negotiate on their own behalf and not be a go-between for the top and bottom levels. In his book, *Middle Power,*[18] Oshry describes a middle manager who had seen his job as making the system work and preventing the top and bottom ranks from destroying one another.

"He had shuttled regularly back and forth between the Elite and the Outs, bearing messages, mediating, negotiating, cajoling, explaining, and justifying each group to the other, trying to be fair to both, feeling very responsible for keeping the system together and making it work, persevering in the face of abuse from both the Elite, who complained he wasn't doing enough to bring the Outs into line, and from the Outs who regularly accused him of being a 'company man,' a sellout who failed to deliver on promises, a powerless messenger who couldn't make decisions on his own."[19]

Oshry's suggestion is that middle managers get out of the middle when it comes to problem solving and serve as facilitators who help the top and bottom ranks talk directly with each other. He feels middle managers should make it possible for the two groups to work out their problems, not do it for them, although he admits there will be resistance to what other people might consider to be bizarre advice.

Because of their pivotal and linking positions, middle managers must plan careful strategies for vertical and horizontal communication. To be effective, they have to serve as two-way conduits of vital information. And, as in Oshry's example, they also need the skills to help other individuals and groups in the organization improve their communication.

Risk-Taking

Taking a risk means deciding to do something that is new or has uncertain results. Risking means gambling that, when you move from one place or situation or idea to another, good things will happen, not bad. Rather than taking hazardous risks, successful risk-takers go for the calculated risk, taken after they have done their homework, carefully thought through the pros and cons, considered the alternatives, and weighed the consequences. To be effective risk-takers, managers need to know the reward/risk ratio. Is the reward to the organization (and possibly to the risk-taker, as well) worth the risk of losing?

Organizations usually have low risk-takers and high risk-takers. Low riskers or risk avoiders have a need to protect themselves; their decisions are based on not making mistakes. As a result, they willingly take on the easier tasks but only make the tough, complex, risky decisions when pushed, and even then, with great caution. High riskers, on the other hand, worry that an opportunity to try something new might pass them by. They eagerly take on challenges and see the world in terms of possibilities. Most library managers are between these extremes, but they need to be aware that people differ in their willingness to take risks. The line between risk and folly is thin. The key is to learn to take the right risks and to manage them in terms of the organization's goals and direction.

Planning and Goal Setting

Another leadership concern involves the planning and goal setting necessary to fill in the gap between the image or vision of how the library could be and the present condition. Yet planning requires more than discovering where you want to end up; it involves a logical process of anticipation and the deliberate assessment of both opportunities and potential obstacles. Effective planning requires knowledge and information (about both the status quo and projected possibilities) upon which to base the dreams of what the future might be like.

Organizational planning has to be a shared activity, with input from everyone directly involved and also those potentially affected by proposed changes. A library board, for example, could envision expansion of programs and services and begin making policies in order to implement the plan. Before they plunge ahead, however, the board needs to hear from the staff. They might discover that the library director and staff would prefer (and are themselves planning for) a completely different direction. Good planning depends on teamwork and full and open communication among units and between units and levels. Some barriers that can cause plans and goal setting to fail are as follows.

- Planning has not been integrated into the library's total management system. The planning process must mesh with the processes of organizing, leading, and controlling.
- Planning has not involved staff at different levels. Those who will help carry out the plan need to contribute to its formation.
- Managers expect that plans will be carried out exactly as they were developed. Planning is a continuous, dynamic process, reflecting changes taking place both inside and outside of the organization.
- Managers fail to operate by the plan. After their authors have put in long hours and hard work, many plans wind up on a shelf and are ignored from then on.
- Goals are set too high. If the goals cannot be achieved, the manager and staff may not even try to implement the plan.
- Individuals are held accountable for things beyond their control. This comes from setting goals for other people and only causes frustration and discouragement.
- Failure to get commitment. Merely distributing or announcing a plan does not ensure that people will carry it out.
- Failure to communicate throughout the whole process. Everyone involved needs to participate in goal formulation, needs to thoroughly understand the goals and their implications, and should have the right to question, clarify, and challenge aspects that seem inappropriate or unfeasible.
- Failure to orient new staff members. Old-timers have lived with the organization's goals and have internalized them; new employees cannot be expected to grasp the organization plan at once or without help.

Obviously, communication is the key to successful planning. It is the means by which the plan is created, implemented, evaluated, and modified. It is also the means by which people are motivated to work on the plan and are persuaded to follow it. (Planning, especially planning for change, is discussed in greater detail in Chapter 7, "Understanding the Change Process.")

The Art and Skill of Delegation

We have made a distinction between leadership and managing, and now we want to distinguish between manager and worker skills. The difference is clear on a widget assembly line where the workers put parts together and supervisors oversee the process to make sure the parts are put together correctly and efficiently. If the supervisor was once an assembler, keeping his/her hands off the widgets and allowing the actual doing to be done by others may be difficult, particularly without training in how to supervise. The supervisor is often more comfortable managing widget parts than people.

In a library, doing the paperwork for an interlibrary loan could be identified as a worker skill, while hiring, training, and supervising the person doing the paperwork could be called managerial skills. But the work to be done, especially in small libraries, cannot be so neatly segregated, nor is it wise to do so.

Managers should be able to perform some of the tasks and be capable technicians. However, since they can't do it all themselves, and shouldn't, they delegate tasks in order to ease their total burden and give themselves essential thinking time and time to concentrate on priorities and overall results. A less obvious benefit of delegation is that it helps the manager test and measure staff capability and trains staff to take on more responsibility. Skillful delegation helps the manager "multiply" him/herself.

Overdelegation can be a problem if the employee is not ready for the new assignment or if it causes a work overload. This can happen when the manager develops the habit of delegating only those "drudge" tasks which s/he doesn't like to do and saves the "dream" jobs for him/herself. Employees soon tire of drudge assignments. What's more, they are not able to learn and grow under this arrangement of duties. In addition to seeing that a variety of tasks are delegated, managers will get maximum benefit from delegation if they analyze their own strengths and delegate on the basis of weaknesses.

Underdelegation can occur when managers have difficulty identifying and communicating essential features of tasks or goals. Or perhaps they are convinced that they can do the task better themselves ("If you want a job done right, do it yourself!") or are too impatient to train someone else. Habit and inertia are other obstacles to successful delegation.

Proper delegation of responsibility and authority is one of the most difficult lessons to learn, but it is also one of the most important principles of good management. It is sometimes tempting for the new manager to try to show off his/her new authority (and hide a lack of confidence) by requiring overly frequent reports and insisting on checking every detail. In this way, the manager makes extra work for everyone and stifles staff initiative. Managers show that they trust their employees by delegating sufficient authority to carry out the responsibilities without restriction.

One library director greatly improved his own delegation by using a "responsibility chart." He and all of his staff members independently made a list of all the activities they performed. The lists were then compiled into a master chart. Across the top of the chart were spaces for names of staff members; checks indicated who did what. The checks were further refined into P (for primary responsibility) and S (for secondary responsibility). Those with primary responsibility were able to take action on their own, and those with secondary responsibility needed to consult with the director or assistant director first.

A daylong staff meeting was devoted to perfecting the master chart. Duties were realigned when duplication of effort was uncovered. It was determined that some staff members were not performing the right functions for their jobs, and others were carrying too much or too little weight. Many misunderstandings about given tasks were uncovered and resolved. Other benefits from this process were a renewed team spirit and an easier means of clarifying performance expectations for new employees.

Dealing with Changing Worker Values and Lifestyles

"What ever happened to the good old work ethic?" This question is asked by many managers, usually the older ones, who see worker apathy, lack of pride in workmanship, high turnover and absenteeism, and general worker alienation in the workplace. There is evidence everywhere that young people who grew up in the 50s and 60s view employment and their jobs from an entirely different perspective than that of their parents and grandparents.

In the United States we have witnessed an evolution from the "traditional work ethic," in which workers respected authority, did whatever was asked of them, and felt a moral obligation to try as hard as they could, to the "work challenge ethic," in which people are judged by the type of work they do and workers demand interesting, challenging assignments to appeal to their high needs for achievement and autonomy; to the "life style ethic," in which workers are more concerned about their own self- actualization than they are about "getting ahead" in the organization, where work is a means to an end rather than an end in itself, and a primary goal is arranging for time and money with which to pursue leisure-time activities.

These so-called "life stylers," who are entering the work force in increasing numbers, have been greatly influenced by television and the messages it conveys. Since the "Sesame Street" generation is used to a lot of mental, visual, and emotional stimulation, they expect the work place to be exciting and to offer them involvement and a meaningful role. Today's young workers have higher levels of education and expectations and cannot be motivated by the same incentives that organizations used to use.

Complicating the picture in the 1980s are the millions of unemployed, underemployed, and dissatisfied workers (primarily women, minorities, and young people) who are waiting to take jobs if they become available. But not just any job. Witness how many menial, undesirable, or "dead end" jobs cannot be filled.

IMPLICATIONS FOR LIBRARY MANAGERS

How do these changing worker values affect library managers and their styles of managing their employees? We see three particular areas in need of change.

1. New and more flexible leadership styles are essential. The authoritarian, who manages with one-way communication and one-dimensional order-giving is becoming increasingly obsolete. Managers can no longer get by with managing the way they were managed. And the organization's communication must reinforce that.

2. In view of the growing diversity among potential workers, how employees are selected and placed takes on added importance. Library managers need to look not only at the position to be filled but also at the kind of person who will best perform the tasks and who will best fit in with the present team.

3. Organizations need to take a new look at the incentives offered to employees, with the realization that different value systems require different motivation. Traditional work ethic people will continue to respect money and power and may only need resources and instruction to succeed on the job. Work challenge people won't do well in routine, repetitive assignments but will respond in a work environment free from excessive structure and where participative decision making and job enrichment projects are available. Rigid working hours and status-related reward systems will not appeal to life stylers. Better incentives for them are the use of work teams, flexible working hours and dress codes, and time-off bonuses. Discovering the need for such incentives and communicating them effectively are essential managerial skills.

ORGANIZATIONAL CONCERNS

Closely linked to leadership and management are the following three special organizational concerns.

Climate

Organizational climate has been used to describe the feel of the work place. What is it like to work there? Stormy? Calm? Cold? Although the climate is intangible, made up of many interacting forces, it is something actually felt by members of the organization and certainly something that influences their morale and productivity. (The physical environment of the library is not considered as an aspect of climate; climate in this sense refers to psychological factors. The physical environment, including the use of space, furnishings, signs, and color will be discussed in Chapter 5, "Critical Communication Skills," in connection with nonverbal communication.)

One library staff set a specific goal to improve their climate for both workers and patrons. They decided they wanted to change from their focus on subject matter, with impersonal, formal, reserved, and nontrusting overtones, to being people-centered, caring, warm, informal, intimate, and trusting. They found the accomplishment of their goal had to take place over time but that they enjoyed the process. The key, once again, was communication. The whole staff had to work at changing their communication patterns and styles. They developed more open flow, easier access for everyone, and even encouraged the expression of feelings. People learned how to listen better and how to test for understanding.

Although they obviously cannot do it singlehandedly, managers are the principal factor in the setting of organizational climate. Becker recognized organizational constraints and the needs, values, and expectations of workers as contributing to climate but added, "the practices of the manager have been proven to be the most important and dramatic determinant."[20]

Perhaps the very best climate a manager can develop is one that gives employees enough freedom and sufficient resources to be creative, almost as if they are working for themselves. The main components of this kind of managerial climate are (1) supportiveness, (2) participative decision making, (3) trust, (4) confidence, (5) credibility, and (6) openness and candor. Notice that all of these components are bound up in and are products of the manager's style and system of communication.

Control

The purposes of control are to keep the organization on a preplanned course and dispel sources of disharmony. This requires a constant flow of information which is reliable and current so that the organization's course can be plotted and, if necessary, corrected.

The amount and method of control to exert in the organization is an important managerial decision and one that needs constant reevaluation. The decision about what needs controlling must, of course, come first. How the exercise of control is communicated will reflect the manager's style and personality. Do controls come via reprimands or suggestions or joint evaluations?

Culture

Organizational culture can be defined as a pattern of beliefs, expectations, and norms shared by the people in the organization. Just as with national or ethnic cultures, the unique characteristics are easier to see from the outside; since cultural norms are taken for granted by the people whose beliefs and behavior brought them about, people inside the culture may not be aware of the dimensions of their own culture. Inside an organization, a new employee might be surprised to be told, "No, not like that. We don't do it that way around here." The new staff member has just tripped over an invisible rope that marks one of the cultural boundaries.

If the manager is having difficulty getting a new plan implemented, it may be because it goes contrary to the group's culture. One large corporation had to move out of its expensive new building because the architect and company planner had not understood their own corporate culture. Workers were used to an informal atmosphere, open space, free access to each other's offices, and the communal coffee pot. The new building had formal arrangements with many doors, and coffee was available only on certain floors. Productivity went way down before they were able to diagnose the problem: their surroundings conflicted with their culture.

It is important for managers to understand the culture within which they are working in order to capitalize on its virtues and avoid clashing with its values. One way to track down a culture is to notice what is rewarded. For instance, some organizations make pronouncements about the importance of creativity, yet innovations are subtly discouraged and only the tried-and-true concepts bring applause. Management By Objectives (MBO) has failed in some organizations because their cultures did not reward a bottom line approach.

Communication provides the link between culture and climate. A positive climate is usually associated with a clearly defined culture. A negative climate can develop from unclear or misunderstood norms.

Messages that run counter to cultural norms will not get through or will arrive in distorted form. One of the reasons that new employees, and particularly new managers brought in from the outside, have difficulty getting new projects implemented as quickly as they would like is that they have not yet identified nor learned to fit in with the organization's mission, its policies, and processes—in short, its culture. Each manager must develop a management philosophy and system that reinforces and supports the organization's desired cultural values. Otherwise, confusion and friction will make consistent progress difficult, if not impossible.

To summarize: In addition to the traditional managerial functions, library managers must also be concerned about their organization's climate, kind and amount of control, and overall culture. These factors affect and are intertwined with the organizational communication.

NOTES

1. Rudi Klauss and Bernard M. Bass, *Interpersonal Communication in Organizations* (New York: Academic Press, 1982), pp. 2–3.

2. Selma Friedman, "Where Employees Go for Information (Some Surprises!)," *Administrative Management* 42 (9) (September 1981): 73.

3. Richard Emery, *Staff Communication in Libraries* (London: Clive Bingley, 1975), pp. 174–79.

4. Marilyn Rehnberg, ed. *Self Assessment Guide for Staff Communication* (St. Paul, MN: Office of Public Libraries and Interlibrary Cooperation, 1984).

5. Gerald M. Goldhaber, *Organizational Communication,* 2d ed. (Dubuque, IA: William C. Brown Company, Publishers, 1979), p. 338.

6. Goldhaber, pp. 350–51.

7. Norman D. Stevens, *Communication Throughout Libraries* (Metuchen, NJ: The Scarecrow Press, Inc., 1983), p. 47.

8. Jean Tague, "Computer Potential for Management Information," *Canadian Library Journal* 36 (5) (October 1979): 268–70.

9. Kenneth E. Dowlin, *The Electronic Library* (New York: Neal-Schuman Publishers, Inc., 1984), p. 61.

10. Joseph McDonald, "Aspects of Management Information and Making Decisions," *Drexel Library Quarterly* 17 (2) (Spring 1981): 61–76.

11. A. G. Kefalas, "Organizational Communication: A Systems Viewpoint," in *Readings in Interpersonal and Organizational Communication,* 3d ed., by Richard C. Huseman, Cal M. Logue, and Dwight L. Freshley (Boston: Allyn and Bacon, Inc., 1977, pp. 25–43). (Chart appears on p. 41.)

12. Douglas McGregor, *The Human Side of Enterprise* (New York: McGraw-Hill, 1960).

13. Peter Drucker, *The Practice of Management* (New York: Harper & Row, 1954).

14. F. E. Fiedler, *A Theory of Leadership Effectiveness.* (New York: McGraw-Hill, 1967).

15. Paul Hersey and Kenneth Blanchard, *Management of Organizational Behavior: Utilizing Human Resources.* (Englewood Cliffs, NJ: Prentice-Hall, 1977).

16. Warren Bennis, "The Four Competencies of Leadership," *Training and Development Journal* 38 (8) (August 1984): 14–19.

17. A. Earl Shorris, *The Oppressed Middle: Politics of Middle Management* (Garden City, NY: Anchor/Doubleday, 1981).

18. Barry Oshry, *Middle Power* (Boston: Power & Systems Training, Inc., 1980).

19. Oshry, p. 27.

20. Charles E. Becker, "Deciding When It's Time for a Change in Organizational Climate," *Personnel* 52 (3) (May–June 1975): 25–31.

Part II
People Working and Communicating Together

Introduction

In Part I of this book, communication was considered in general, organizational terms. In Part II, the focus shifts to interpersonal communication as it occurs within that larger context. Chapter 4, "Interpersonal Communication within the Library," deals with relationships and transactions between individuals, particularly the "one on one" variety, as well as the conflict that may result, for which communication can be both a cause and a cure. Chapter 5, "Critical Communication Skills," discusses the most important skills needed by both senders and receivers, including the intrapersonal skills of thinking and reasoning and the often misunderstood qualities involved in sending and receiving nonverbal messages. Finally, Chapter 6, "Small-Group Communication," looks at the additional skills and knowledge necessary to communicate effectively in small groups.

Chapter 4
Interpersonal Communication within the Library

Libraries are composed of groups of people who are linked together by communication, both person to person and group to group. Although some of these linkages have formed more by accident than design, and some are difficult to trace because of their ephemeral nature, all such connections are the foundation of the organization's internal, interpersonal communication.

RELATIONSHIPS AND HOW THEY AFFECT COMMUNICATION

Information networks in an organization evolve over time from patterns of use as well as from need. Connections between people who are linked through a formal or an informal communication network (or both) may be strong or weak, open or closed, heavily used or ignored. Pattern variations stem not only from work-related factors, such as organizational or task requirements, job function, and status level, but also from the kind and quality of interpersonal relationships that have developed.

Obviously, we like and are drawn to some people more than others. We are attracted to people whose beliefs, attitudes, and values are similar to our own. We enjoy being around people who give us positive feedback or in some other way make us feel good. We are more apt to associate with people who stimulate us or give us energy rather than people who, for any reason, irritate us or deplete our energy. Depending upon our own personality, conditioning, and personal preferences, we may be drawn to or repelled by people who are warm and outgoing, have a bizarre sense of humor, are quiet and shy, or who are highly analytical.

Research has also borne out the fact that interpersonal liking and friendship increase with knowledge of and experience with each other. In other words, strangers are more difficult to like and/or be comfortable with until we get to know them and begin to share perceptions, meanings, and, therefore, understanding and appreciation. The more time we spend with someone, the more apt we are to learn to like him/her.

All of these factors (and a myriad of others) influence and shape interpersonal relationships, which, in turn, influence interpersonal communication. The depth and quality of the relationship have a direct bearing on the kind and amount of communication that occurs between people.

For example, staff members who have a close, trusting relationship will probably communicate a great deal, sharing much and withholding little, regardless of each person's official need for the information. Many grapevine transmissions are made on this basis. By contrast, staff members whose values clash or whose personalities are not "in sync" will probably communicate the barest minimum and even that may be incorrect, incomplete, or distorted. This will reinforce their distance and lack of mutual understanding.

Although they don't usually do it deliberately, some staff members may develop such strong personal networks that persons outside of the network find their incoming messages are consistently too few and too late. People who complain about not being "in on things" would do well to pay more attention to developing and nurturing their relationships. In libraries with managed organizational communication, the inadvertent playing of favorites (which can seriously affect the direction or amount of communication flow) can be spotted and corrected. The importance of the relationship/communication connection is a fact of organizational life that can never be completely eliminated. Nor should it be.

Person to Person

Interpersonal communication refers to the messages that are sent and received between people. At this level of communication, an individual deals with, encounters, confronts, and exchanges meanings with others—usually on a one-to-one basis.

The old-fashioned approach to teaching interpersonal communication was to concentrate on "public speaking," focusing on the speech (significance of content and effectiveness of organization) and the speaker (performance skills such as vocal projection and use of gestures). Although these skills are still worth learning, we now know that placing the entire emphasis on the speaker meant that one-half of the equation was left out. The proper focus for interpersonal communication, then, is not so much on how the speaker is performing but on what the listener is understanding.

Effective dialogs and interpersonal interactions depend upon two important aspects: (1) establishment of an open, supportive climate and (2) effective communication.

The Need for an Open, Supportive Climate

The previous chapter in this book discussed climate in terms of overall atmosphere throughout the organization. Here the discussion is narrowed to the climate established between individuals that can encourage or discourage interpersonal communication.

When you share things about yourself, or your reactions and perceptions of the other person, you are being open. As two people find an increasing number of things that they can share in mutually helpful ways, trust develops between them. True, some things may not be appropriate or relevant to that relationship. When inappropriate things are shared, or shared ideas seem to be used in hurtful ways, trust and openness decrease. Some risk is always involved when we try sharing a new kind of information in a particular relationship. Openness (which is the opposite of defensiveness) implies a commitment. When two people have a mutual concern for helping each other grow and the communication skills necessary for accurate perception and understanding of each other's ideas and feelings, then additional areas for sharing gradually become appropriate.

Building or maintaining an open or supportive climate calls for (1) making statements that are descriptive rather than evaluative or judgmental, (2) adopting a problem-solving orientation rather than one of control, (3) making comments that reflect empathy and honesty rather than a withdrawn neutrality, (4) building equality in the relationship rather than power struggles, and (5) maintaining a willingness to look for options rather than an either/or approach that sees only one alternative.

The Need for Effective Communication Behavior

The specific communication skills of reading, writing, speaking, and listening will be discussed in Chapter 5, "Critical Communication Skills." Here we will look at some of the general responses and behavior that people use in interpersonal transactions, as well as ways they can be improved. The following ideas are adapted from categories developed by Carl Rogers.[1]

- **Evaluating.** Implies a judgment on respondent's part as to goodness, rightness, appropriateness of speaker's problem or point. Example: "Your approach to that problem was all wrong." Evaluative statements can harm a relationship, especially if they are not balanced by positive "strokes"; evaluative statements may be helpful if and when we are asked to make a value judgment.
- **Interpreting.** Respondent tries to tell the speaker the reason for his/her problem and what should be done about it. Example: "You feel that way because of what happened at the

meeting yesterday. You should call another meeting." People rarely welcome being told why they have a problem or what to do. Yet interpretive statements can lead to growth and insight, provided they are presented as hypotheses about the other person's behavior, not as self-evident fact.

- **Supporting.** Respondent tries to reassure, soothe, boost morale, find agreement, and offer strength. Example: "I know you can do it!" Supportive statements can be helpful if the speaker needs acceptance before tackling the problem, but when overdone, cheerleading and pep talks are irritatingly patronizing.
- **Probing.** Respondent seeks further information, opens other avenues, offers other alternatives, viewpoints. Example: "How did you feel when that happened?" Probing statements can help clarify the actual problem or introduce aspects the speaker had not considered, but when pursued too far, they begin to sound like badgering or cross-examination.
- **Understanding.** Respondent seeks only to clarify his/her perception of the speaker's points, feelings, and meaning by paraphrasing and perception checking. Example: "Am I right in sensing you aren't sure why you got the reaction you did?" Understanding is the most likely response to promote trust and genuine interest, but the major barriers to mutual understanding are overworked and often unthinking tendencies to evaluate, interpret, support, and probe.

Feedback

Giving and getting accurate and helpful feedback is essential to making interpersonal communication effective. Feedback (either verbal or nonverbal) serves to acknowledge receipt of a message and to check the accuracy of the transmission.

In face-to-face communication, almost continuous feedback is possible and desirable. The sensitive communicator is alert to all clues that will tell him/her how the listener is reacting. By continually monitoring the listener's response, the speaker can and should modify the message. Even the intent or goal of the communication may need to be revised according to the feedback received.

So far, this section has focused primarily on what is known as external feedback; that is, information you receive. There is another dimension, however, which is known as internal feedback. Internal feedback is in operation when you begin to reflect about something you have just said and realize that it isn't clear. You may say something like "Let me put that another way." Of course, these two types of feedback are at work simultaneously, and each often affects the other. Effective communicators are also effective listeners of what they themselves say. By listening to our own messages, we may decide it is desirable to change what we have said.

When we speak to another person we expect a response. This anticipation results from internal feedback that causes us to expect a certain behavior to occur. Internal feedback is at work when we correct what we intend to say before we say it on the basis of what we think will be the response of the listener.

Interviews

The interview is an important form of communication which involves two or more people in an intimate setting, at least one of whom has a definite communication purpose. Examples are an employment interview or a reference interview. All persons involved both speak and listen. Further, an interview is a conversation with a predetermined purpose, which usually involves the asking and answering of questions. Interviews may be for the purpose of getting or giving information, or both. The communication in an interview is different from that of other face-to-face interactions in that it focuses on specific information and attempts to eliminate extraneous messages.

To be successful, an interview must involve participants who collaborate in seeking and giving information pertaining to a common goal. Effective interaction is necessary to accomplish the goal, and as we have said before, effective one- on-one interaction depends upon the building of a relationship and rapport.

People may be understandably uneasy at the beginning of an interview. The interviewer, therefore, has the responsibility of greeting the interviewee and communicating in a way that demonstrates that s/he will be treated courteously and that there is no need for defensive behavior. The setting is important; it should afford as much privacy as the nature and purpose of the interview require. Also, wherever possible, physical barriers such as desks or tables should be removed, as they increase feelings of distance or tension. For some library personnel with limited space, moving the interview out of the office might be the best idea.

Interviews are usually classified as either directive or interviewer-centered or nondirective or interviewee-centered although a combination is also possible. In the directive interview, the interviewer usually initiates the communication and controls the subject and the pacing. Although the interviewer also controls the nondirective form of interview, the control is less obvious because the questions are open-ended and the conversation more free-flowing.

Often misunderstood, the word "control" leads many to believe the interviewer should completely dominate the interaction. On the contrary, control does not mean manipulation of the interviewee, or doing all the talking, or slavishly following a predetermined outline.

Rather, it means moving the interaction along to accomplish the purpose within the time available, keeping on track, but also allowing flexibility and whatever degree of informality is appropriate to the occasion and purpose.

An example of a directive employment interview follows.

Librarian: I see you have had considerable library experience.

Job Applicant: That's right.

L: What exactly were your major responsibilities in your last library position?

JA: Primarily, I handled interlibrary loans, but I also filled in for the reference librarian.

L: What aspect of library work do you think you do best?

JA: I particularly enjoy helping patrons and I believe I have a lot of "people skills."

L: That sounds good. Now tell me what you don't like doing.

Example of a nondirective interview:

Librarian: Tell me about yourself.

Job Applicant: Well, I don't know where to begin. (There is a pause, during which the librarian remains silent.) I was born and raised in Illinois. We lived on a farm and I went to small rural schools until I went away to college.

L: I see.

JA: I got interested in library work when I took a class in library science at college. Then I got a work study job in the college library and really liked it. So I decided that I'd become a librarian and maybe some day be a director of a large library like this one.

L: What do you like best about yourself?

JA: Well, let's see. I guess I like my energy and ambition and ability to work hard.

Stewart and Cash identify the advantages and disadvantages of directive and nondirective interviewing as follows[2]:

Advantages	Disadvantages
Directive:	
Easy to learn	Inflexible
Takes less time	Limited in variety and depth of subject matter
Provides quantifiable data	Limits interviewer's range of techniques
Can be used as supplement to questionnaires, analyses, and observations	Often used to replace more effective and efficient means of collecting data
Nondirective:	
Can deal in-depth with wide range of subject matters	Time-consuming
Allows interviewer more flexibility	Requires psychological insight and personal sensitivity
Provides interviewer opportunity to establish ongoing relationship with interviewee	Usually generates nonquantifiable data

THE REFERENCE INTERVIEW

As all librarians know, the reference interview may not always fit the descriptions or classifications of "typical" interviews. For example, the reference librarian controls the information, but it is the patron who initiates the interview and controls the subject. Reference librarians often have to use a probing technique and "play detective" in order to provide the assistance the patron wants. Here is an example:

Reference Librarian: May I help you?

Patron: I'd like to see some law books.

Reference Librarian: Is there a particular aspect of law that interests you?

Patron: Well, I guess it would be the courts, the court system.

Reference Librarian: Could you tell me anything more specific about what you'd like to know about the courts?

Patron: I want to know how the Small Claims Court operates in this state.

Reference Librarian: Fine. Now I think I can help you.

THE SKILL OF ASKING EFFECTIVE QUESTIONS

To a large extent, the quality and depth of information you will be able to gather as an interviewer depends upon the nature and timing of the questions you ask. Effective questions serve two vital functions: First, they stimulate the interviewee to share information, and second, they provide the interviewee with guidelines about the kind of information being sought.

Open questions call for broad, general answers, which can go in many different directions, while closed questions elicit specific, short answers such as "yes" or "no." For example, a staff member says, "This overtime is a pain in the neck. I don't mind a little of it, but it should be spread around more. Some of the other staff don't get picked half as often as I do." If the interviewer responds with, "It sounds as if you feel you have been treated unfairly in the assignment of overtime. Would you tell me more about that?" s/he has asked an open question. Such a question mirrors the feelings inherent in the staff person's statements. On the other hand, suppose that the interviewer asks, "How often did you work overtime last month?," s/he has asked a closed question which requests specific data. Of course, the closed question may be just the right one to use, depending on the purpose of the interview and who initiated it.

In addition to open and closed questions, two other basic kinds of questions are available to the interviewer. One is the primary question, which is used to introduce a new topic or to direct the discussion into a new train of thought. The other is the secondary question, or probe, used to further develop the information asked for by a primary question when the primary question elicits an incomplete or unclear or otherwise unsatisfactory answer.

Consider the following dialog between Harriet, a library manager, and George, her assistant. Pay particular attention to the quality of the questions asked.

Harriet: George, I'd like to ask you a few questions about our new filing system.

George: Sure, shoot.

Harriet: Well, my first question concerns the new system as compared to the old one. Do you think the new system is better?

George: Oh, sure, definitely. It's a big improvement.

Harriet: I'm sure glad of that. Have you had any problems with it?

George: Oh, a few so far. But we found the errors without much trouble.

Harriet: Then the rest of the staff are happy with it?

George: I think so. Nancy and Tom have been complaining about a few things, but the program is sound.

Harriet: Great. I'm glad everything is going so well. Appreciate your help, George. Keep me posted.

George: Sure will. See ya.

Obviously, this is an ineffective interview. The manager failed to receive the information she needed because of her poor questions and because she did not follow up or probe the inadequate responses. Harriet asked only primary questions and either didn't notice or decided to ignore the clues that George was giving in his answers. Of course, it could be that the manager didn't really want to know, and if that was the case, she met her objective. Failure to probe effectively is one of the major causes of ineffective interviewing.

A skilled interviewer avoids questions which lead the interviewer to a particular answer. Contrast the following questions: "How do you feel about having all the staff go on flextime?" and "You wouldn't say that you are for flextime in the library, would you?" Not only is the second version a highly leading question, but if it is asked of a subordinate by a superior, the expected answer can almost be guaranteed.

THE IMPORTANCE OF LISTENING

We will discuss the skill of listening more thoroughly in Chapter 5, "Critical Communication Skills," but before leaving the subject of interviewing, we must at least call attention to the vital role listening plays in all interviews. All too often, training programs for interviewers stress the skills of talking and asking questions without explaining that listening may really be the more important skill. Transcripts of many managers' interviews indicate that they tend to fill the majority of the time with what they have to say, while interviewees are limited to brief responses to direct questions. This tendency is verified by Steinmetz:

"Studies substantiate the fact that the average supervisor, while gathering information, will talk up to 85% of the time. Although they do talk most of the time, *they don't think they do.* One study disclosed that a group of managers who had, in fact, talked 90% of the time, felt they talked no more than 50% of the time."[3]

Perhaps one reason interviewers talk more than they should is that many of us are uncomfortable with silence. A lull in the conversation leads many of us to say something, anything, to get the discussion going again. Silence, however, is a useful tool for interviewers. It indicates that the interviewer is waiting to hear more and it can increase the comfort level of those interviewees who take a little longer to formulate their thoughts.

Although professional interviewers accurately record what is said, this does not mean that they write excessively during the interview. In fact, writing should be kept to a minimum. This is true for several reasons: It is distracting to both parties and often causes the interviewer to stop listening while trying to sort out the notes; pauses for writing tend to chop the interview into disconnected parts; and the notes are based on the writer's impressions at that particular time and may not be an accurate evaluation of the whole. The best rule seems to be to concentrate on listening during the interview and make summarized notes at the end.

Interviewers must not only listen, they need to *show* they are listening, with good eye contact and appropriately encouraging responses. This is not only to be courteous but because speakers do a far better job of communicating when they feel they have the listener's attention. Imagine the effect on the interviewee, who is probably already under stress, if the interviewer is looking out the window or at some papers on the desk. Even though the interviewer may really be listening, it can appear to the interviewee that the other person is not interested in either the speaker or in what is being said.

USING CONFLICT CONSTRUCTIVELY

Conflict is both the boon and the bane of people who work together. Conflict is a boon because it is the best means of stimulating provocative ideas, creative solutions, and zestful interchanges. Conflict becomes a bane, on the other hand, because it requires skill to make it constructive rather than destructive, and it calls for courage to face up to the problem and work through to a resolution.

Conflict can be defined as a struggle between opposing perspectives, such as a clash or divergence of opinions, interest, or aims. In their definition, Frost and Wilmot add some important dimensions:

"From a communication perspective, *conflict is an expressed struggle between at least two interdependent parties, who perceive incompatible goals, scarce rewards, and interference from the other party in achieving their goals.*"[4]

They point out that a conflict that exists in only one person's head is an intrapersonal conflict, within the person, but the delineation of interpersonal conflict requires that the people involved both perceive and express the struggle. They add: "It is through communication behavior that conflicts are recognized, expressed, and experienced."[5]

Note also Frost and Wilmot's use of the term "interdependence." Conflict cannot take place in a vacuum. The people involved in any conflict must have a stake in the outcome and must perceive that their opponents have the possibility of interfering with or changing the outcome they are working for. If the parties to the conflict were not interdependent—if each side's actions didn't have consequences for the other side—there wouldn't be any conflict. So conflict disputants need each other, perhaps only to keep the conflict going, but more positively, to work toward a mutually satisfactory resolution.

Conflict is absolutely vital to productive interactions. Why should we waste our time agreeing that the sky is blue or that two plus two equals four? It is only when we disagree about something—when we look from different perspectives or when we make different interpretations—that there is really anything to talk about. Just as life would be dull if it were all placid and free of tension, so too are conversations where everyone agrees with everyone else about every subject, or worse yet, pretends to in order to avoid conflict.

Despite our need for conflict, many of us have been taught to be "nice" and avoid conflict. Our conditioning tells us to steer clear of controversial subjects in the interest of peace and politeness. True, nobody loves the individual who argues about everything, but there is also no one more boring than the "Pollyanna" who thinks everything is just wonderful; and there is no one more harmful to a good discussion than the self-appointed peacemaker who tries to smooth over every disagreement just when it is getting interesting.

Uncertainties and tensions seem to keep people on their toes and functioning better; solving problems provides a sense of accomplishment. When problems defy our efforts at resolution, however, we become depressed and frustrated.

Conflict is not only beneficial, it is inevitable. As Rizzo puts it:

> "Conflicts and the conditions that cause them occur in every organization or group; they are an inevitable consequence of human interaction. Managers and other employees should never interpret conflict as failure, for often it is not. It simply arises out of the complex problems and interdependencies that exist in organizational life."[6]

CAUSES OF CONFLICT

Think back to your last experience with conflict. Perhaps it was a forthright, out-and-out battle with someone. Perhaps it was merely an uncomfortable feeling that all was not well between you and another person or a group of other people. No matter how serious or complex the conflict was, try now to analyze what brought it about. This is not always easy to do because of unconscious or subconscious feelings, opinions, or values. We may not always be sure of the sources or causes of the conflicts in which we find ourselves.

Do you remember an occasion when you took an instant dislike to a person you were seeing for the first time? Perhaps the person reminded you of someone else you disliked; perhaps the way the person moved or was dressed triggered some stereotypical reactions you have to a group or class of people; or perhaps the person's reputation had preceded him/her and you had formed an opinion based on comments made by other people.

Conflicts can be caused by differences in perception, beliefs, values, and general ways of looking at life and the world. A classic example here is the optimist versus the pessimist. Conflict can be caused by scarcity (one job for 10 applicants) and by turf battles. Harry may be director of only one unit of the library, for instance, but Harry sees his part as the total, and he wants to make it as important as possible. Territorial disputes, coupled with limited resources, are a major contributor to interpersonal conflicts in organizations.

Sometimes the real reasons behind a conflict are hidden, particularly when people's egos are threatened. Powell and LeLieuvre describe what happened when one of them visited an elementary school library and learned that students were being sent to the library as punishment. Since only a paraprofessional was on duty in the library at the time, the author called the city supervisor of elementary school libraries to complain. The supervisor agreed with the criticism, thanked the author for reporting it, and promised something would be done. Later, the author got an angry call from the school principal, who was upset because he had been bypassed. He felt he should have been told rather than the supervisor. As it turned out, the principal was not interested in solving the problem, in fact, he didn't think there was a problem. He was only interested in protecting his place in the chain of command.[7]

Other causes of conflict are struggles for power, status, or control; pressures to conform; unclear or divergent goals; disagreement over the best methods to use to achieve the agreed-upon goals; and differing labels or meaning for the same concept. In summary, there are an infinite number of possible causes of conflict just as there are unlimited numbers of unique, distinct, and varied human beings. Generally, conflict causes are rooted in either situational or personal determinants.

Assertion versus Aggression

For those people conditioned to avoid conflict there has seemed to be only one alternative to being passive and "nice," and that was to be aggressive or "nasty." However, the concept of assertiveness offers a happy medium between the two extremes.

The intent of passive, nonassertive behavior is to avoid conflict; the intent of aggressive behavior is to dominate or control; the intent of assertive behavior is to communicate. Passive behavior is based on the hope that the problem will go away but that if it doesn't, indirect manipulation might get your point across. Aggressive behavior is aimed at getting your way at someone else's expense. Assertive behavior is a clear statement of what you want and what you will and won't do. Here's an example:

> You're about to leave your office to go to an important meeting when the phone rings. It is Sally, a colleague in another department who starts to tell you about a problem she has been having with the library's children's program. You are anxious to get off the phone. You say:
>
> 1. "Uh huh, I see," while you listen...and listen. (Non-assertive: accommodation of the other's needs at the expense of your own. Your excuse to yourself is that Sally is a friend and you don't want to hurt her feelings. But at the moment, you don't like Sally or yourself.)
> 2. "Look, I'm too busy to talk to you now. I've got more important things to do than listen to some little problem of yours." (Aggressive: disregard of the other's wishes and feelings. Your excuse to yourself is that Sally should be told off for always assuming that you want to hear about her problem or that you have nothing better to do. You momentarily feel good about "getting it off your chest," but soon you feel guilty, frustrated, and alone.)
> 3. "I'd like to hear more about it later. I was just on my way out to a meeting when you called. I'll call you back this afternoon, okay?" (Assertive: direct statement of facts and wishes. You feel good about being clear and honest, while at the same time taking the other person's needs into account.)

Assertiveness is appropriately exercising the right to stand up for yourself; to feel, think, and act in ways that enhance your sense of self-worth and personal integrity without violating the rights of others. It calls for honest, straightforward communication. Assertive individuals take responsibility for their own actions and contributions; rather than avoid conflict, they analyze their role and/or responsibility, weigh the effects on themselves and others, and (when necessary) confront the other people involved and try to solve the problem.

During the interpersonal exchanges that occur while people are working out the conflict, assertive comments are by far the most effective of the three approaches. Such comments do not "dump on" or accuse the other person nor do they invite anger or hostility that often result from passive, doormat behavior. Assertive statements give other people the benefit of the doubt and are as objective as possible.

Understanding Power

Who exerts influence over whom? Who listens to whom? Whose suggestions get carried out more often?

Power is the capacity to affect or control the behavior of another person or group. Power is more of a potential than a concrete reality. If I perceive that you have the power to block me from achieving my goals, then you are, indeed, powerful.

Power is, of course, a relative quality. In most organizations, power is of a social rather than a coercive nature. We are more concerned about power *to* than power *over*. We allow ourselves to be influenced because we like the influencer or want to be liked by him/her. The attractive, articulate person appears to have an innate power over others. But conflict can easily occur when the innate power of some is resented by others or when it appears that the power is being misused. The "haves" and the "have nots" in a power context are invariably poised on the edge of conflict.

Status and power have to be earned. They are conferred on someone, not grabbed. Two major sources of power in organizations are position and personality. If your position gives you the ability to hire and fire personnel and control budgets, you have built-in clout or power. Not all high-level or high-sounding positions have power, however. Staff positions in support functions have less power to influence the organization's main mission than line positions do. What's more, you may have authority to decide a particular issue, but you may or may not have the power to enforce the decision. Person power comes from likeability and attractiveness. If people like and respect you, they will want to follow your suggestions and do what you say. Of course, the stars of any organization are those few who have both position and person power.

You may find you have power without having sought it. Perhaps your status or expertise or knowledge cause others to defer to you. Even though you have a middle- or lower-level position in a library, if you have some information or skill needed by others, you have a certain amount of power. Demonstrations of power may be subtle or outright. One way to understand the power structure in your organization is to pay attention to the people sought out when others want to know what is really going on or when they want to make sure that something is done right.

If power is jealously guarded or abused, the organization is ripe for eruptions of conflict. If people have the notion that power is scarce and has to be fought for, conflict is inevitable. The truly powerful people, on the other hand, don't have to flaunt their power. They build teams and share power because they know that their own power is enhanced the more they empower others. According to Hugh Prather, "Power lies in the release from fear, not in the attempt to provoke it."[8]

Each person in a conflict has some degree of power which is a product of the environment and the relationships involved. By examining the power dimensions of a conflict, it is possible to open up new options for resolving the dispute.

COPING WITH CONFLICT

How we feel about conflict determines how we will attempt to handle it. Do we find it zestful and exciting or evil and frightening? Is winning the key to us or is it more important to turn the other cheek? Thus we can see that our personal tendencies and values create a predisposition to handle conflict in habitual coping styles.

People usually deal with conflict in one or more of the following ways:

- Avoidance. Under stress, our bodies gear up for either fight or flight. Since the outcome of fighting is highly uncertain and the process full of risks, many of us opt for withdrawing as the better part of valor. We may cover up our leaving the scene by shifting the focus to logic or analysis, or we may try to dilute the conflict by calling it a "simple misunderstanding."
- Smoothing. "Let's be polite. Let's all be one big happy family." The focus here is on surface harmony and getting along. Some of us go out of our way to accommodate, to play down differences.
- Reliance on Authority. "If we can't resolve this ourselves, let's go by the policy manual or give it to a committee or the boss."
- Compromise. "The fairest way to divide up the budget is right down the middle. You give here and I'll give there." Each gives up something in order to meet in the middle.
- Problem Solving. "Let's see if we can figure out a way to give us both at least some of what we want." "Let's attack the problem instead of each other." We focus on collaboration and work for the best possible solution.

Although problem solving has the best chance of creating equitable and long-lasting solutions to most conflicts, the other coping styles are sometimes useful. For instance, if you find yourself in the middle of two other people's conflict, and you decide it isn't really your problem, withdrawing may be the very best action to take. Similarly, referring the problem to an authority may be recommended. Why waste time haggling over a problem if there is already a policy in the books that will settle it?

On the face of it, compromise appears to be a neat and logical way to resolve a conflict. However, what appears to be logical and fair may not solve the problem. Take the case of the couple who goes to the movies. He's far-sighted and she's near-sighted. So they compromise and sit in the middle where neither can see. Or the "fair" method of chopping the budget in half may not be fair at all if one department is larger or has greater needs.

Negotiating Conflict Resolutions

Perhaps the best of all methods to cope with conflict is to follow a process of negotiating. What is negotiating? It is a give-and-take process between people where both sides have interests and needs. It is a process where both parties maneuver, each with the purpose of gaining the best possible advantage. A key ingredient is flexibility—maintaining a range of options and fall-back positions—with emphasis on the give as well as the take. Some people who think they are negotiating are really making demands. Taking a fixed, inflexible position is the opposite of negotiating.

Negotiation takes place at high levels, such as those involved in international disputes or hostage situations. But it also occurs in day-to-day dealings. Whenever someone has something you want or is preventing you from getting what you want, offering to negotiate is your best option.

The emphasis in negotiation has been on winning, on defeating your opponent, on making the best possible deal. But for most of us, the context in which we are negotiating is important. We very often are negotiating with someone we care about, in a relationship that we don't want to damage. We might win the negotiation but feel terrible if it caused us to lose a friend. And what is the likely outcome if we win a negotiation that "one-ups" the boss?

So what works best is a negotiation that aims at a win/win outcome, where the needs of both sides are taken into account and met as much as possible. If both sides gain a resolution that they can live with that doesn't put anyone down or make anyone wrong, the solution is far more apt to succeed.

In a win/win negotiation, both sides have some interests that are shared and others that are opposed. (We sometimes forget or downplay the shared part.) An example of how the process could succeed would be in a performance appraisal. Both the boss and the employee stand to gain from the employee's doing a good job because the better the job, the more the organization benefits. Both share an interest in clear communication between themselves and in understanding the employee's goals for job improvement. Only one area of opposed interests needs to be negotiated: translating the employee's performance into a salary increase, which the employee wants to be sizeable and the employer wants to keep small because of budget restraints.

Another area in which negotiation can be used to work out an interpersonal conflict is that of misunderstood roles or behavior. A very enlightening task, for instance, is to write out your own job description—not for you, but for your successor. In other words, list only those functions needed to be performed by the person in this position, disregarding what you like to do or actually do. Then ask your boss to write a job description covering the functions s/he feels are needed in the job, regardless of who holds it. When the two of you sit down to compare notes, there may be some surprising revelations. If different functions or priorities have surfaced, they need to be clarified and negotiated.

PERSONALITY CLASHES

It is true that some people just cannot get along with each other; and there are even people who can't seem to get along with anyone—least of all with themselves. Yet far too many problems are blamed on personality conflicts, probably because other causes of conflict are more difficult to diagnose. We seldom take the time to find out the reasons for the behavior of grouchy or uncooperative colleagues. Instead, we write them off or work around them. Turner and Weed suggest some alternatives:

> "We may notice that supervisors and workers who are difficult to get along with and who cause conflict on the job are likeable and easy-going away from the job. One might ask the logical question, If the cause of the conflict is the individuals' personalities, then why are they not difficult to get along with all the time? Other useful questions to ask concern a problem person's beliefs: Does the person think that the way he or she is doing the job is the way it has to be done or should be done? Are there some understandable reasons for his or her beliefs? Is the person frustrated? These questions suggest that there must be something in the work situation that causes the problem."[9]

Because each person has a unique set of attitudes, beliefs, and values, conflicts can indeed occur frequently between people of opposing views. Usually, the conflict will escalate as one person insists on winning the other person over to his/her belief. Conflicts would be easier to solve if the individuals involved didn't have to be right or if they could enlarge their view to accommodate the possibility that they are both right.

Strangely enough, organizations that provide a welcoming, supportive climate for many different kinds of people with many different viewpoints will have fewer interpersonal conflicts. They have learned that conflict is only one possible outcome when differences are integrated. And, according to Likert and Likert, when conflict does occur in this kind of group, it is treated as a permissible, resolvable difference of opinion.[10]

The cultural norm for such an organization goes something like, "Honorable people can differ and it's possible to disagree without being disagreeable." When people are lucky enough to be part of this type of environment, relationships are built on the premise that everyone is entitled to be different and that being different is acceptable, valued, and won't interfere with two people working together.

COMMUNICATION AND CONFLICT

Communication is very often what gets us into conflict in the first place, and it can also be what keeps the conflict going or resolves it. If the lines of conflict become rigid and set, polarization can occur. When two people each become convinced that "truth is on my side," differences that may have once been slight now grow to extreme proportions.

When polarization occurs, communication is both the problem and the solution. The term "breakdown in communication" is used when people either miscommunicate or stop communicating; yet the solution is usually more communication. But increased communication may intensify rather than reduce conflict; it may even contribute to and help exaggerate the polarization. More communication may open new avenues for dispute and result in even more upsetting information.

Yet communication, honestly and skillfully executed, can be the means of resolving even the most deep-seated of antagonisms. Here are some ways that communication can be used to resolve conflicts.

- Look at the language used. What do we call our conflict? People call it the way they see it. If the person with whom you are in conflict sees it as a disaster, a standoff, or a battle royal, you can bet s/he will act accordingly. Try to change your opponent's perception of the conflict by labeling it your way. Call it a challenge or an opportunity for change, or at the very least, call it *our* problem.
- Try some in-depth listening. We know that listening is especially difficult when we are emotionally involved or our egos are on the line. Instead of listening, we are apt to be framing

our next rebuttal. In the midst of conflict we need to listen with intensity, resisting all distractions, by tuning in to what is being said and what is not being said. We need to separate what is being said from the way in which it is being said. Whenever a person is talking, messages are being sent both verbally and nonverbally, and communication is taking place at both levels. The best listener listens at the same time to different levels and decides what the message is that the speaker is trying to communicate at that time.

- Check your perceptions. In addition to listening and trying to figure out what the person means, it is frequently important for us to play back to the person what we are hearing him/her say because our own emotions and defense mechanisms filter what we hear. "Do I understand what you are saying is..." opens the door for clarification or amplification. The other person may respond, "Yes, that's right," which shows you have listened well. Or the other person may say, "No, that's not what I meant," which may begin the process of explaining where the conflict comes from or even begin to defuse it.

- State your opponent's case as fairly as you can. This demonstrates both your listening skill and your attempt at objectivity. If you can add an additional argument and make his/her case even stronger, you can turn a heated tirade into a rational debate and break through the polarized logjam.

- Send "I" messages rather than "You" messages. "I" messages tell how I feel, how I perceive, or how I respond to a situation, rather than "You" messages which imply blame or accusation. "Boy, you sure said a dumb thing!" only succeeds in getting the other person's defenses up. Contrast that with, "I feel uncomfortable when you say things like that." The second version gives the other person feedback which s/he may or may not use, but it also gives the person the freedom to give his/her perception of the statement and explain without having to fight you because you made an accusation.

- Look carefully at the person you are communicating with. If you sense from facial expression or body shifting that you are not getting your message across, paraphrase what you have said or ask the other person to paraphrase. Describe your own feelings to help others decode your nonverbal signals. Ask for feedback. Don't assume understanding.

- Clarify goals and purposes. Are both sides clear on what they want? Have criteria been established against which proposed solutions can be checked? Do both sides know what a good resolution to the conflict will look like?

- Look for and stress common ground. There are always aspects that people can agree on and recognizing that two

people are together on some points gives them a foundation upon which to build.
- Try making fewer assertions and offer more hypotheses. Example: Instead of saying "The planning committee should be abolished!" say "I wonder what would happen if we disbanded the planning committee?"
- Compartmentalize the issue by breaking it into subpoints so you can tackle one at a time. This is especially useful if the issue in conflict is too complex for easy resolution.
- Get help. Communication and conflict management skills are hard to learn. Most require practice and coaching, as well as the breaking of long-standing habits and patterns. Feedback from a trusted friend or colleague is very helpful. On-the-job help from internal or external consultants can prove beneficial. A qualified third party can provide fresh perspective and establish ground rules for working through even the most well-established conflict situations.

Communication skills are essential to deal effectively with conflict in order to make the most of what it offers by constructively channeling the ideas and energy that result and to successfully negotiate and resolve differences. Good communication reduces the fear and anxiety that often accompany conflict situations.

NOTES

1. Carl Rogers, *On Becoming a Person* (Boston: Houghton Mifflin Company, 1961), pp. 329–37.

2. Charles J. Stewart and William B. Cash, *Interviewing: Principles and Practices* (Dubuque, IA: William C. Brown Company, Publishers, 1974), p. 9.

3. Lawrence L. Steinmetz, *Interviewing Skills for Supervisory Personnel* (Reading, MA: Addison-Wesley Publishing Company, Inc., 1971), p. 36.

4. Joyce Hocker Frost and William W. Wilmot, *Interpersonal Conflict* (Dubuque, IA: William C. Brown Company, Publishers, 1978), p. 9.

5. Frost and Wilmot, p. 10.

6. John R. Rizzo, *Management for Librarians: Fundamentals and Issues* (Westport, CT: Greenwood Press, 1980), p. 214.

7. Judith W. Powell and Robert B. LeLieuvre, *Peoplework: Communications Dynamics for Librarians* (Chicago: American Library Association, 1979), p. 169.

8. Hugh Prather, *A Book of Games: A Course In Spiritual Play* (Garden City, NY: Doubleday & Company, Inc., 1981), p. 108.

9. Steve Turner and Frank Weed, *Conflict In Organizations* (Englewood Cliffs, NJ: Prentice-Hall, Inc., 1983), pp. 19–20.

10. Rensis Likert and Jane Gibson Likert, *New Ways of Managing Conflict* (New York: McGraw-Hill Book Company, 1976).

Chapter 5
Critical Communication Skills

This chapter will examine the specific skills that are essential to both interpersonal and organizational communication. Since every purposeful communication starts with a thought, thinking and reasoning act as the foundation for all the other skills. This chapter will look at the two sending skills—speaking and writing—and the two receiving skills—listening and reading. Finally, those pervasive phenomena which make up nonverbal communication are examined, along with Neurolinguistic Programming (NLP).

THINKING AND REASONING

Since the dawn of consciousness and the first attempt at problem solving, humans have been both fascinated and baffled by the thinking process. For a long time, no one knew for sure exactly what went on in the brain when people tried to analyze or interpret or decide from among several alternatives. It seemed impossible for the brain ever to understand itself. In recent years, however, many breakthroughs have helped us understand the brain more fully, neurologically, chemically, and structurally. For example, we now know that the brain can produce its own pain-killing drugs in the form of endorphins; that specialization occurs between the brain's right and left hemispheres; that Alzheimer's disease causes the brain and its functioning to deteriorate. Brain research is a rapidly changing and expanding frontier.

The first (of 20) definitions that one dictionary offers for the word "think" is: to have a conscious mind, to some extent capable of reasoning, remembering experiences, making rational decisions, etc. (That "etc." is still another clue that it is difficult to come up with an all-encompassing definition.) Reasoning is usually defined as the process of forming conclusions, judgments, or inferences from facts or premises.

In one sense, thinking is everything that goes through our minds. In another sense, thinking is using memory machines. When we call human behavior "intelligent" we mean that some kind of prior learning is a necessary condition for thinking to take place, and we also mean that thinking is restricted to what goes beyond what can be directly observed through our senses.

John Dewey, in his monumental work, *How We Think,* first published in 1910, made the point that people usually do *not* think as long as events are running smoothly. We allow habit, impulse, mood, and routine to get us through work and play. It is only when the routine is disrupted that we are forced to think. Dewey distinguished between random recollections and half-developed impressions, on the one hand, and what he called reflective thinking, on the other. He wrote that reflective thinking required both a sequence of ideas and a consequence or conclusion.[1]

The process of thinking results in a commitment or a personal resolution to do, or to cease doing, some act; to adopt or to reject some opinion; to anticipate doing something; or to adopt or to reject some objective. Whether our thinking is done intrapersonally (inside our own heads) or interpersonally (in association with other people), it results in what we commonly call ideas. These ideas are the substance of what we seek to transmit when we communicate.

The quality of thinking depends on how well-informed we are and how well we can select and use information. But even if we make a decision based on all of the available facts, it won't necessarily be the "right" decision. Being human, we sometimes have to make decisions based on incomplete data. What's more, we sometimes draw the wrong conclusion. For example, a person may weigh all the facts s/he can get before accepting a new job only to later discover a conflict of values with the new boss which outweighs all of the positive factors.

It is also possible for us to possess many facts in one area but few in others. We may make the mistake of assuming a person is an expert in all fields merely because that person is famous or has been elected to high office. If the correctness of a decision is not a measure of the effectiveness of our thinking, just what are the indicators then? Two key aspects of effective thinking are reality-testing and probability-estimating.

Reality-testing is the process of checking out what is real—what is consistent with the "real world" around us. It involves separating fact from fancy, tradition, and opinion. It includes perceiving and evaluating the current situation and relating the data to past knowledge and experience.

The process of probability-estimating occurs when we have alternative solutions with which to deal and can estimate the probable consequences of the various courses of action open to us. Inasmuch as reasoning involves going from the observable to the unobservable, we are confronted with the problem of predicting the likelihood that our reasoning is correct. This means that reasoning tries to establish the probability that subsequent experience will confirm the truth of our inference.

THINKING AND LANGUAGE

Despite an obvious connection between thought and written or oral language, there is disagreement about the exact nature of the relationship. Some feel that speech and thought are identical, that the process of thinking is like talking to yourself through the use of "inner speech." Some proponents of this view go so far as to claim, "If you can't say it, you can't think it." Another position in this debate is that speech and thought are closely related but are separate elements of a single process. A third perspective is that language is only the expression of thought and is, therefore, not essential to thinking.

Although we cannot resolve this difference of opinion, one thing upon which we, as communicators, can agree is that thought seems to have little purpose until and unless it is expressed. When we broaden the definition of language to include such nonverbal signs as gestures and images, it is clear that language is necessary for both thinking and communication.

We have all had the experience of becoming much more aware of something once we have a name for it. For example, we may be used to seeing sparrows at our bird feeder and have the impression that they all look pretty much alike. Once we learn to distinguish tree sparrows from the others, however, we are amazed at how many tree sparrows "start coming" to the feeder.

Words have the ability to preserve and apply specific meanings to what we think about. In addition, through the use of words in sentences, meanings can be organized in relation to one another. Words and sentences are the tools of thinking. Obviously, the larger and more accurate our vocabulary is, the better able we are to think and conclude because thinking is never more precise than the language it uses.

CREATIVE THINKING

Jarring us out of our habitual responses is the goal of those seminars, books, and speakers that advocate and attempt to teach creative thinking. Most advocates of the creative approach feel that we are all born with this ability but that our environment, our conditioning, and our schooling cause a gradual inhibition and loss of the spark.

Pioneers like Alex Osborne and Whitt N. Schultz developed techniques such as brainstorming and the encouragement of imagination that have been widely learned and applied. A more recent advocate is Edward De Bono, who developed the notion of lateral thinking. According to De Bono, most of us have been taught vertical thinking (the traditional, logical method used in science and mathematics). Vertical thinkers move forward, step by step, toward a solution, and each step must be correct. In contrast, lateral thinking may jump from point to point, using a zigzag pattern, without worrying about logic or being right. Vertical thinkers dig the hole deeper; lateral thinkers find a different place to dig the hole.[2]

Roger von Oech calls these same two functions "hard" and "soft" thinking. He feels that both have their place, with soft thinking being the most effective in the germinal phase when searching for new ideas and hard thinking being best for narrowing and evaluating ideas.[3]

Although the parallels are not exact and the research findings are far more complex than a surface comparison justifies, we cannot help but call attention to the similarity of vertical/lateral and hard/soft distinctions to generalizations made about the left and right hemispheres of the brain. For example, here is what Wonder and Donavan write:

> "Problems of communication, listening, memory, management, organization, stress—these are the dilemmas facing American business. Increasingly, business is recognizing that they cannot be solved by logic, discipline and attention to detail alone. They require not only these traditionally valued skills, but also intuition, free-spirited invention and comprehension of the overall picture. In other words, we must learn how to draw on both the left side of the brain, home of logic and efficiency, and on the right side of the brain, home of intuition and inspiration."[4]

When people compare the brain to a computer, they have found a good analogy—but for only half of the brain. The "left brain" (binary skills) functions somewhat like a computer, sequencing information, arranging it in logical categories. Coulter compares the left brain to a computer and the right brain to a hologram (a three-dimensional photograph recorded on film by a reflected laser beam). She makes another important point:

> "Most of the focus in education has been directed toward development of this binary processing. Information is arranged in logical sequences, divided into step by step segments and presented to students in a pre-planned order. Nearly all textbooks, curriculum guides and lesson plans are based on this logical developmental arrangement of information...."[5]

Both in and out of the education field, thinking has generally been considered a process that goes on, more or less by itself, instead of a subject that could be taught and learned. The author of *Brain Power,* Karl Albrecht, wrote in *Training,* that "The focus has been almost exclusively on teaching *what* to think, rather than *how* to think"; he continues:

"How many of us have fallen prey to the same subtle messages transmitted to students by the structure of our academic curricula: the notion that each person comes into the world with a certain basic capability for thinking and learning and the only thing a teacher or school can do is help that person acquire a storehouse of information? How many of us unconsciously consider thinking ability more or less innately fixed and assume that, except for a bit of fine tuning, we can never significantly increase that ability?"[6]

As our educational systems react to increasing knowledge about the brain and the process of thinking, more emphasis should be placed on teaching students how to think. Less emphasis should be placed on I.Q. testing and other arbitrary, imprecise classification schemes in favor of helping students improve their skills of concentration, logical reasoning, recognizing patterns, and making inferences.

In the meantime, what are the significance and implications of the thinking process for librarians? Certainly, it is not the librarian's place to try to help patrons avoid fallacious thinking; the librarian merely provides the information, or tools, with which the patron can think and conclude. But what about the library supervisor's staff? Accusing someone of reasoning errors or not being logical is a below-the-belt blow to the ego because everyone thinks s/he is a rational, reasonable human being. Helping someone improve thinking abilities, by example or by coaching, can be done, but it requires patience and tact.

Matching preferred thinking styles and work assignments is another suggestion. For example, staff who are "concrete" thinkers will probably be more comfortable organizing material into logical patterns, based on vocabulary identifiers rather than by idea. "Abstract" thinkers, on the other hand, will enjoy helping patrons, and they can deal with multiple problems at the same time.

Is the library strictly a left-brain world? Must it be? Of necessity, books and materials are arranged in a "logical" order. This aspect will only increase as more and more libraries shift to formal computerized methods of access and storage.

Perhaps the librarian's major contributions can be: (1) to recognize that what have been identified as left- and right- brain skills are overlapping and (2) to encourage and reward the use of right-brain skills among both staff and patrons. For example, the library's atmosphere need not be hushed and grim. Humor and playful spontaneity have their place. Also the library's physical appearance can be geared toward enhancing creative thinking. For example, whenever a library display is clustered around a theme, people's right brains will be stimulated.

In addition, the way the library is arranged and decorated can be visually and sensually artistic and colorful, with emphasis placed on round and irregular shapes and splashes instead of the linear. (A more detailed discussion of this takes place in the "Using Nonverbal Messages" section of this chapter.)

There is a direct connection between our ability to think and our ability to communicate. Whatever we learn or do to improve one cannot but help improve the other.

THE SENDING SKILLS

Speaking

The most obvious of our communication skills, the one we appear to be using most of the time, is our ability to verbalize. We may be informally talking with only one other person, as in an interview, or we may be formally addressing a large audience, but we know the outcome we achieve is not only the measure of our communication; it is also an important means by which we are judged professionally. Although most of us actually spend more time listening than speaking, the act of listening is less apparent and the outcome more difficult to measure.

The communication process is basically the same whether we are speaking to one or many. The information goes from one head (the speaker) to one head (each individual audience member) at a time. When we speak of "mass" communication we mean that one speaker is transmitting to many people at one time, but the communication is not received by a "mass" but by individuals. Although the process of transmitting and receiving information is the same, experienced public speakers know that their organization, their style of delivery, and their audiovisual aids need to be adapted for different audiences. For example, smaller audiences are able to respond to subtle, intimate, and low-key speaking styles. Larger audiences require more of a "performance" with broader gestures and emphasized points.

Once a speaker has a subject in mind, s/he should next determine the *purpose* for speaking. What does the speaker want the listener to do, think, or feel as a result of the presentation? The stimulus behind making such a presentation may be external (the library director wants a report) or internal (an urge to share a piece of news). In both instances, the motive for speaking could be quite varied: We want to show how much information we have; we want to enhance our prestige; we want to help solve a problem; or we want to influence other people's understanding or behavior.

The motive for speaking should not be confused with the purpose. Motive is an expected personal benefit or satisfaction derived from speaking; purpose, on the other hand, is related to the desired response to be elicited from the listeners. Most speech purposes fall into one or more of the following categories:

Purpose	Desired Listener Response
1. To entertain, to make people feel good	favorable attention, laughter
2. To inform, instruct, or clarify	understanding
3. To stimulate listeners to believe or feel something	intensification of already held beliefs
4. To persuade, convince, or change attitudes	decisions about or commitment to new ideas
5. To actuate, to get people to act or change actions	specific action

Although it is not necessary to orally identify the purpose in the actual speech, it should be kept in mind during the preparation. Otherwise intelligent decisions about content or organization or style cannot be made, and the end result may be a confused audience who has no idea of what is being communicated or why.

Both speakers and writers benefit from analyzing their prospective audiences ahead of time. The more they can learn about the audience (what is the age range, knowledge of subject, feelings about the subject and about you, etc.?), the more tailored the presentation can be. In addition, speakers profit from finding out about the occasion (why is the meeting being held?) and the place (what is the size and shape of the room?) in advance. If it is not possible to do this analysis prior to the presentation, there are some ways to gather information during the speech. Observe verbal and nonverbal reactions during the introduction and while speaking; ask questions; ask for a show of hands about some aspect you plan to deal with; plan activities to involve the audience.

The major reason that face-to-face interactions are the most accurate is that the speaker receives instantaneous feedback and has the opportunity (some would say the obligation) to adapt the message on the basis of the audience's response. Without this adaptation, speakers are merely up in front of a group, talking to themselves.

Most of the feedback that comes from listeners is nonverbal and, unless the audience is well-known to the speaker, difficult to read. Of course, if most of the audience is nodding off or fidgeting, the message is fairly clear. But a frown on the faces of one or two people may or may not be a message to which the speaker should respond. In any event, the "meaning" of the frowns is ambiguous. Perhaps the frowning listener cannot hear well, has a headache, needs new glasses, or disagrees with what the speaker is saying.

When nonverbal clues are scarce or unclear, effective speakers cannot assume that the "message" is directed at them or that they know what it means. Instead, they must engage the audience in an oral question-and-answer exchange or a general discussion to get a better reading. (Nonverbal communication will be discussed in greater detail in the "Using Nonverbal Messages" section of this chapter.)

Some speakers present their ideas in a "stream of consciousness" mode, saying them in whatever order they occur in their mind. This rambling method, in which all of the ideas appear to carry the same weight and significance, is very confusing to an audience. Speakers will find their audiences listening better (and remembering longer) those ideas which are presented in a recognizable organization pattern. For instance, if you are asked to give a speech about the history of the library, a chronological pattern, starting with the date of founding and moving through events to the present, would be a natural approach. If you are giving a presentation to the city council on the library's need for increased funding, you might use a problem-solution format in which you discuss the problems of rising costs and increased patronage and evaluate some possible solutions, demonstrating that the most feasible solution is increased funding.

Organization patterns need not be confined to formal outlines. With even a minimal ability to draw, the speaker can develop a "mind map," which can be used both to help the speaker prepare and the listener to grasp and retain. For example, a tree shape could be used to illustrate the aspects of a problem, from its roots to its branches. Or a bowl of fruit could be used to describe the organization (the bowl) and its policies (pieces of fruit). If speakers draw mind maps as they speak, they are not only providing themselves with a useful outline to keep themselves on track, they are also providing the audience with an effective visual aid.

The use of humor often makes the difference between an outstanding and a so-so speech. But be careful with how you use humor, lest it work against you instead of for you. A joke dragged in on the theory that it will relax the audience seldom works. The anecdote or humorous description needs to make a point—and a point that is relevant to the speaker's topic and purpose—in order to be effective.

Despite careful planning and organizing, some speakers are held back by a bad case of podium panic or stage fright. Giving a speech is listed most often as the number one fear by individuals, even more than fear of death and fear of flying! When asked what they're really afraid of, most people would say they fear appearing dumb or foolish. It may be discouraging to stage fright sufferers to hear that even the most experienced speakers are nervous before an important presentation. Three additional ideas may be more helpful: (1) Nervous energy is a positive factor because it shows that you want to do a good job and you are "up" for the task; (2) signs of nervousness are far less obvious to an audience than a speaker imagines; and (3) the best speakers are audience- and message-conscious rather than self-conscious and think of themselves as a medium through which ideas are being channeled rather than the focus of the audience's attention.

Nervousness that gets out of hand can affect a speaker's credibility; nervousness under control will not. One way to control nervousness is to plan ways to use the excess nervous energy. Build in movement as a part of the speech: Write on the chalkboard, hold up something, move around as you speak. Don't forget to breathe! Long, deep breaths before you begin to speak can calm the nerves and lower the voice; deep breathing also increases the amount of air needed to project the voice to the back row.

Writing

If you asked the average person what kind of writing s/he does on the job, the response would probably be, "only what I have to." For many, writing has always been an unpleasant chore. Even answering a simple letter may be traumatic for some.

One reason that writing is feared is that it has a permanent quality and is there for others to look at. If we make a grammatical mistake or the words come out in awkward clumps, it is there on paper for people to see and judge us by. Because of this, our writing tends to take on a formal and flowery quality and we are apt to use big words and long, complex sentences. The result is stilted or jargon-filled language rather than communication.

As with a speech, writers need to prepare for writing a report by deciding on a purpose, analyzing their prospective reader(s), and organizing the material into an effective pattern. Another problem that writers share with speakers is the difficulty of getting and holding attention. Even well-written material will fail to inform, influence, or persuade if the reader's mind is on something else.

Think about your own reading habits. Since you don't have time to read every word of every piece of paper that floods your desk, you have learned to identify the material you don't have to read (now or at all) and also the kinds that can be skimmed or stashed away for later, more careful reading. Picturing the stacks of paper on your own desk can make you a more effective writer because you will learn to be brief and to the point and because you understand the need to catch and hold the reader's attention.

Too many business letters sound as if they could have been written by anyone and were intended to be read by anyone. They are impersonal, routine, and dull—stranger writing to stranger or machine to machine. Others contain so much verbiage they appear to be written to impress rather than express. What a pleasant feeling it is to receive a letter that seems to have some thought behind it for the person who will read it. Contrast this with the countless letters that sound as if the writer simply went to the files, pulled out a previously written form letter, and updated it with fill-in-the-blank information.

Tailoring the message to fit the recipient ensures attention. Skillful tailoring means that the reader can tell immediately why s/he got the letter, what's in it for him/her to read it, and what thought or action is expected from the reader.

Report writing is perhaps the most difficult writing task; whether formal or informal, routine or special, reports have significance as essential management tools. Managers use reports as instruments of control, to detect defects or problems in organization structure and functioning, and, above all, as the basis for decision making. Reports measure performance against planning, control costs, provide reference and documentation, and coordinate activities of scattered segments of an organization.

Usually longer and more complex than other written communications, reports take up large blocks of managerial and staff time. Their bulk and scope make them more difficult than memos and correspondence.

Writers who routinely grind out reports may forget that the purpose of the report is to answer a question or solve a problem. As communications to patrons, employees, or management, reports focus on providing facts and supplying new information.

Another aspect that sets reports apart involves the slow feedback reponse; word comes back even more slowly than for other forms of written communication. Reports take longer to research, write, reproduce, and distribute, as well as to read and respond to or act on. Budgets and other constraints may prevent reports from being acted on quickly. Report writers, therefore, must keep potential delay in mind. What effect will elapsed time have on the data included, the words chosen, and even the mailing list?

Before deciding whether and how to write a report, you need once again to consider your potential readers. Do they need the information? Will they use it? Will they read the report conscientiously or just skim it? Levels of interest and need vary among report readers. Why labor over details that go unread?

To find out what their managers wanted in engineering reports, Westinghouse staff did extensive surveys and came up with some startling responses. Their managers reported that they all read report summaries but that only about 60 percent read the introduction, and slightly more than 50 percent read the conclusions. Even more surprising is that less than 25 percent read the *body* and only 15 percent read the *appendix.*

When busy managers read report summaries, they wanted to know immediately what the report was about, including its significance and implications, and the action called for. If the managers saw the report summary as relevant, they may then go on to read the introduction and body. Reasons given by managers for reading more than the summary were that they were (1) especially interested in the subject, (2) deeply involved in some aspect of the project, (3) sure that the problem was urgent, or (4) skeptical of the report's conclusions. Report readers didn't like to have to hunt for the answers to such questions as what should be done, how much would it cost, and what courses of action are available.[7]

The significance of these findings for report writers looms large. Technical and detailed matter must be written in terms of the reader and his/her projected use of the material. Most readers want only the essence, not the details. Put key backup information in the appendix and save the rest for those few who will ask for it.

Professional writers regard their first drafts as raw material and operate on the assumption that editing and rewriting will always be necessary to shore up any first, primitive effort. This approach frees writers from worrying about providing high-quality reports the first time around; instead they are free to just put the ideas down as quickly as they come, using double or triple spacing for later editing. However, standards must increase with each revision, which often means large chunks of material will eventually be deleted or radically changed.

Of course it is painful when you have to decide that a clever turn of phrase doesn't add to the sense or the flow of the report and, therefore, must go. But the pain eases at the sight of a well-rounded, yet economically lean, paragraph or page. Sentences that are neat and concise, as well as accurate and clear, more often result from rewriting than from writing.

The four main purposes for editing are (1) to improve organization; (2) to improve clarity and readability; (3) to remove mistakes in grammar, spelling, and punctuation; and (4) to polish and improve the writing style. Some writers like to edit longer material four different times, for each of the four purposes.

In any case, don't skip the editing process. Think of the poor impression the reader gets of the two companies whose communications we recently received. The writer of one, a plumbing and heating firm, offered to restore our "piece of mind;" the other writer, at a utility company, began a printed enclosure letter both ungrammatically and nonsensically, "As one of our customers, we recognize that for you to get the most out of your service ...."

THE RECEIVING SKILLS

Listening

Of the four sending and receiving communication skills, we spend most of our time listening, and yet that is the skill that is weakest in most individuals. Research shows that most people listen at 25 percent efficiency. That doesn't mean they actually heard 25 percent of what was said; that means that of what they heard, they got 25 percent of it right. That is a scary statistic when you consider how much of our education is acquired through hearing (lectures and discussions) and how much of the work of the library is done through oral transmission (instructions and interviews). It's possible that much of what we thought we learned correctly may turn out to be completely erroneous.

It is easy to believe that listening is a task and skill that requires little practice and effort to perfect. Indeed, as long as listening is regarded as a passive activity, such as being aware of background music, there seems to be no need to work at tuning in to other people. But try really listening to the music, to follow the harmony, counterpoint, melodic themes, and pick out individual instruments, and the task becomes more difficult. So, too, does listening require a similarly active effort if we are to fully experience the meanings of what people are trying to communicate.

We have our first listening lessons as infants, as we try to make sense out of the noises all around us. As small children, first trying to talk, we quickly spot the connection between speaking and listening, and we learn both how to talk and how to listen by imitating the behavior of the people around us. It is in this period when many of us pick up bad listening habits. The child who has to beg for attention gets the message that listening is not very important because s/he is seldom listened to. The child whose elementary school teacher goes over and over the same material gets the message that s/he doesn't have to listen because the lesson will come up again.

Adults as well as children have short attention spans when it comes to listening. Most of us listen in spurts, paying attention for a few seconds, then tuning out. Because we can all think faster than most people speak, we find we have spare thinking time. What we do with that thinking time highlights the difference between a good and a poor listener. The poor listener will use it to think about something else, perhaps daydreaming or preparing a rebuttal to what the speaker is saying. The good listener recognizes that people hear with their ears but listen with their minds so that effective listening requires concentrating on listening and resisting distractions. What's more, the good listener's spare thinking time is focused directly on the material being listened to. For instance, the effective listener will use the spare thinking time to (1) evaluate the material, (2) review the main points that have already been made, and (3) try to predict what's coming.

Since most of us have never been taught to listen in any formal way, we listen well enough to get by, without realizing that, with some effort and practice, we could greatly improve our skills. Memory experts say that one of the most important reasons for poor memory is failure to listen. Listening, in fact, is not an isolated skill but a package composed of intelligence and memory as well as listening. The more intelligent you are, the better you can listen for relationships instead of to isolated bits and pieces of information. The better your memory, the longer you can remember the material listened to.

No communication is ever complete until there is understanding on the part of the listener. Proper listening is active, not passive. It is a positive attempt to concentrate and examine what is being said, not a neutral or withdrawn attitude that says, in effect, "Just see if you can catch my attention and make me listen. See if you can get through my passive deafness." The important thing is to be attentive, not just try to look attentive. We have all learned that listening attention is easy to fake; all we have to do is look at the speaker, smile or nod occasionally, and we can give the impression that we are fascinated when in truth our minds may be miles away.

Certain attitudes often get in the way of our listening effectively. One attitude is thinking about the speaker's motivations and intentions. Another is thinking for the speaker by mentally trying to direct what the speaker should be doing, thinking, or feeling. Yet another attitude is thinking ahead—completing the other person's thought before s/he has a chance to finish it. Of course, the most helpful and productive listening attitude is thinking with the speaker—simply trying to understand the speaker's message, and the feelings and viewpoint behind it. This is the only attitude that truly aids in understanding.

Here are some ways to improve your listening:

- Practice listening whenever you have the opportunity. When you find yourself in an audience or in front of the radio or television, and the subject does not excite or even interest you, use the time to exercise your mind and improve your listening. Say to yourself, "If I really listen to this speaker, I'll bet there will be at least one good idea I can use." Play listening games with your children or friends, where each player has to answer questions about material just listened to.
- Give and ask for feedback as a part of listening to complex material. Even the best of communicators will occasionally misinterpret the spoken word; it is important, therefore, to ask clarifying questions such as, "Do I understand you to mean ...?" As simple as this process is, some people don't use it because they think it insults the speaker's intelligence. On the contrary, such requests assure the speaker that you want to make certain you have listened well and understood the intended meaning. Rather than ask for clarification or verification, too many listeners try to work things out for themselves, often with costly results.
- Try to listen from the speaker's frame of reference. Get on the same wavelength. Critical listening demands that you be continually on the alert to pick up all of the signals and that, in addition, you try to listen between the lines—listen for what is not said as well as what is said.
- Listen for concepts and main ideas rather than for facts and figures. If we start with the premise that even the best

listeners cannot listen to and remember everything, we are more effective by trying to identify the most important ideas and avoid getting bogged down in details.

- Listen fully and fairly to the message and try not to be influenced by the package it comes in. As humans, we have a tendency to discount or ignore messages that contain poor grammar or are delivered in an unpleasant voice. Of course, the status and credibility of the speaker cannot help but influence the quality of our listening. (Emerson said, "Who you are speaks so loudly I can't hear a word you are saying.") But good listeners work hard to get the message and try not to be sidetracked by the way in which it is delivered.
- Listen actively by asking clarifying questions and feeding back to the speaker what we understand s/he is thinking and feeling; this also requires that we refrain from giving advice or criticizing the speaker. Too often, when someone comes to us with a problem, we immediately tell the person what should be done or what we did when we had a similar problem. Instead, we should first make sure we understand the nature of the problem and, especially, whether our advice is being sought. Most people would prefer to have us listen empathetically and allow them to think through to their own solution.

Reading

The second receiving skill is reading. Since the very nature of libraries is to provide reading materials, and since most librarians choose the field because of a fondness for reading, it seems wildly presumptuous to discuss the skill of reading in a book for librarians. Nevertheless, the subject is included here, first, because it is a key receiving skill, and second, because there is too much to read today and too little time to read every word of it, and third, because the librarian may be asked to help a patron or staff member improve his/her reading skills.

Reading is easier than listening in two ways. First, we can read at whatever speed is comfortable for us, and second, if our mind wanders, we can go back and reread. With listening, on the other hand, we must adjust to the speaker's pace, and there is seldom the opportunity to hear the same material twice.

People differ widely in their reading abilities. The range is much broader than that which exists in speaking or in understanding speech. One difference is the rate or speed with which we read. One person may read a book in three hours while another may take 20 or more. Another difference is in comprehension of what is read. You can tell whether it takes you a minute or 10 to read a page. But can you always tell whether you have successfully understood the author's meaning? You may think you have and be mistaken. Improving reading skills does not necessarily mean increasing the speed. Sometimes the solution is to slow down the fast and careless reader.

Deciding what (or whether) to read is usually the first step in the reading process. Picture yourself arriving back at your desk after a three- day absence. In a hodgepodge pile are letters, reports, magazines, advertisements, memos, and bulletins. You pick up the top piece of paper, which happens to be a letter. How do you decide whether to read it now, throw it away, or put it in the "read later" stack? Most people quickly analyze four basic factors before making that decision.

1. First impression. At a glance, you take in the overall appearance of the page. Is the material short or long? Does it have an attention-getting opener? Does it have eye appeal? Does it look interesting?
2. Relevance. Next, you look for the key idea and try to figure out what it has to do with you. You ask yourself, "Do I need to read it? Will it make me smarter? Happier? Will it give me a change of pace in a pressure-packed day? What's in it for me?"
3. Purpose. Most readers will then try to determine the author's purpose, asking themselves such questions as "Why was this written? Why was this sent to me? What is expected of me—is this letter providing straight information or do I have to do something?"
4. Author. "Who wrote this?" is another question the reader's preliminary glance tries to detect. "Do I know him/her? Is it somebody important or influential? Is it somebody with credibility? Or is this just a form letter from a nameless individual or company?"

If the answers to these four factors are both positive and readily apparent, you now decide whether to read it now or later. Whether you read it now or later, you then must decide whether to read it carefully or quickly.

You have already used one speed reading technique when you preread or previewed the material in order to make the decisions about whether or when or how to read. Previewing is useful to get a general idea of content. People who preview usually read the first few paragraphs in their entirety. Then they read only the first sentence of the following paragraphs. Last, they read the entire last two paragraphs. Previewing doesn't give you all of the details, but it does give a quick, overall view and keeps you from spending time on things you don't need or want to read.

Another selection technique is skimming, which is useful for getting a general idea of shorter or lighter material, as well as a good way to remind yourself about the gist of something you have previously read. Skimming calls for picking out only a few key words in each line. Skimming is not careless, but careful, reading of those portions of the material that are most likely to contain essential information.

Neither prereading nor skimming is effective for full comprehension, but you can pick up at least 50 percent of the meaning with these techniques and that may be enough. People who want to increase both their speed and comprehension do so by learning to read word clusters rather than word-by-word as we were originally taught. This takes practice, of course, but the reward is being able to read more in less time.

Reading aloud for the enjoyment of others is also a skill that librarians may need. Effective oral interpretation lies somewhere between the overarticulation of a Shakespearean performance and the underarticulation of mumbling the minutes of the last meeting. For children's literature, we need some drama and color; for adult literature, we need the ability to savor well-chosen and artistic language. But the feeling that we want to communicate when we read aloud is that of sharing an author's words for both comprehension and appreciation.

Reading aloud is more enjoyable for the audience if the reader maintains the same kind of directness and eye contact that speakers use. To avoid getting buried in the material or having to hunt for his/her place each time s/he looks up, the reader needs to do the following: (1) hold the book or material high enough so that the reader needs to move only the eyes, rather than the head; (2) hold the book in one hand and use the other hand to mark the line being read, with the hand dropping down line by line in the middle of the page; and (3) train the eye to see word clusters rather than each individual word.

USING NONVERBAL MESSAGES

Much has been written about "body language." The subject of nonverbal communication, however, is much broader than visible movements made by the human body. Nonverbal communication includes all of the messages that go along with or instead of words. In learning how to communicate, we have stressed words—how to write grammatically, how to read and spell. We are less aware of nonverbal messages because they have been learned by imitation and by accident and because we respond to many of them unconsciously.

A classic example of the subtlety of nonverbal cues was the experiment Robert Rosenthall did with teachers and students. Rosenthall told some teachers that through a new testing method, he had identified certain of their students who were about to make a breakthrough in learning ability from average to excellent. He asked the teachers not to tell the students. When Rosenthall returned later to the classrooms, his predictions had come true. Only then did he confess that the students had been selected at random, not from tests. The students had been influenced to do better work by the teacher's expectations, communicated by nonverbal clues outside the awareness of both teachers and students.[8]

We receive nonverbal messages through all five of our senses. Think of all the sensual data acquired even in a simple conversation with someone. We *see* facial expressions, body shape, movement and position, hand gestures, eye movements, clothing and grooming. We *hear* tone and pitch of voice and rate of speech. We may even *touch* each other on the arm or with a handshake or hug; at the same time, we might be aware of the feel of the chair or the table surface or the *smell* of perfume or shaving lotion. It's no wonder that words carry less than 35 percent of the meaning in a two-person conversation, while more than 65 percent comes from the nonverbal aspects.

Although we constantly react to the nonverbal messages sent by others, we are in continual danger of misinterpreting their real or intended meaning. With people we know well, we can begin to develop a nonverbal dictionary: A certain expression around the eyes means Brenda is tired; when Carl pushes his chair back, it's because he thinks it's time to end the meeting. But these interpretations, acquired over time, cannot be applied to people you meet for the first time.

For instance, one supervisor began to notice that one of her staff members, who otherwise had a very calm exterior, would repeatedly lick his lips when the tension of a heated staff meeting began to affect him. She used this information as a signal that it would be best to shift attention away from this individual and give him a chance to relax. This was invaluable information for the supervisor. But she was wise enough to know that the meaning behind one person's lip-licking behavior could not be generalized to other people. Another person might lick his/her lips because they were dry, not out of nervousness.

Crossed or folded arms *may* mean that the person is rejecting ideas or withdrawing from involvement; however, such an arm position may also mean that the person is cold, finds that a comfortable way to position the arms, or has a stomachache. One reason that it is risky to generalize meanings is that nonverbal communication is culturally based and certain cues mean very different things to different people. Take the example of the American OK sign, a circle made with the thumb and forefinger. In Japan, this symbol stands for money (round coins); in France, it represents a zero, meaning nothing or worthless; in Malta, Sardinia, and Greece, the sign is an obscene insult.

By far the most powerful nonverbal communication is eye contact and yet this, too, varies by culture. White, Anglo-Saxon Americans equate direct eye contact with honesty and forthrightness. Other cultures avoid eye contact except when either a confrontation or a sexual invitation is involved.

In summary, interpersonal communication can be greatly improved when people become more aware of the subtle nonverbal messages being sent and received all around them, and if they will, at the same time, be very cautious about interpreting the meaning (particularly the intentional meaning) of such messages.

An additional aspect of nonverbal communication that library managers and staff can profit from knowing more about has to do with the library building: how it is arranged and decorated and what this communicates to patrons. A major influence on peoples' perceptions and attitudes toward the library begins outside with the library building itself. Is the building attractive and inviting or cold and forbidding? Does the building need to be painted or have repairs made?

When a prospective patron enters the library for the first time, what is his/her impression? Does the atmosphere say "Come in" or "Don't come in"? Are staff members talking with each other so that the patron has to interrupt with a question? Does the librarian turn aside as someone approaches? Are there bewildering rows of shelves or unmarked hallways and doors leading to unknown areas?

Although it does not come as a surprise to most people that physical settings and color schemes influence human behavior, for a long time there has been too little connection between how architects and designers planned buildings and space utilization and what actually occurred in the finished space. Function has had to follow form. Take the simple problem of people forming a line to check out books. If the checkout desk or counter is long or broad, pushy people may fail to wait their turn, making other people angry or, at the least, uncomfortable. The solution, of course, is to arrange the space so that it is evident where the line is to form and provide barriers or guide ropes so that line jumping is difficult or impossible.

Lucky is the library manager who can participate in the design and decoration of the library. With years of experience and intimate knowledge of the space needs and functions of staff and patrons, librarians can prevent many problems through careful planning. But even so, mistakes can be made that affect both work load and communication. When patrons enter some libraries, they have to go to the main desk to ask about everything, from where to find the card catalog, dictionary, or the reference desk, to where to find the rest rooms. Even if the room arrangement cannot be changed in such a library, at least signs and arrows can be displayed to cut down on the staff time needed to give directions.

Albert Mehrabian studied library environments and decided that most librarians would put books first, people second, and buildings last. He further noted:

"A collection of books is not a library but a warehouse. A library is by definition a place where books are used, and if a library environment is such that the use of books is discouraged, those responsible for administering the library have failed to perform one of their essential functions."[9]

Factors cited by Mehrabian as discouraging the use of books are dreary-looking and inconvenient stacks and floor surfaces that promote static electricity. (He equated the static electricity with classical avoidance conditioning.)

Julian Lamar Veatch, Jr., made a thorough study of factors affecting public library facilities, among them the aspects of access. For example, are doors easily opened, not only by average patrons, but also by children, the disabled, and the elderly? Hard-to-open doors communicate the opposite of public service. Veatch also analyzed library office space in terms of staff needs for privacy, personal space, and territoriality. He defines privacy not as being alone but as being able to control other people's access to you.[10] Needless to say, the most effective environments are those that take into account work flow, time and motion studies, anatomy, physiology, communication patterns, and interrelationships.

Colors not only communicate, they give and take energy. Color is a passive form of energy which people absorb from their clothing and surroundings. According to Mella:

"Science has discovered that certain colors, like reds, raise the blood pressure, speed up the pulse rate, and even increase the rate of breathing. Shades of blue cause the exact opposite, and they lower blood pressure and slow down body activity. Still other medical experiments have shown that variations in the amount of color stimuli profoundly affect muscular control, mental concentration, and nervous activity."[11]

Dramatic changes have been brought about by changing color schemes. For example, pink on prison walls has a calming effect and has reduced violence. A school in Canada brought down absenteeism and the number of disciplinary problems, while at the same time raising the IQ scores of some of its students, by substituting yellow and blue for orange, white, beige, and brown and replacing fluorescent lights with full-spectrum lights. When Dupont discovered that light green reduced eye strain, many libraries, schools, and hospitals incorporated the light green into their color schemes. Unfortunately, light green is not a motivating color and too much light green affected productivity.

Many libraries are painted orange or use furnishings upholstered in orange. Now we know that orange stimulates the appetite and may encourage library patrons to leave in search of something to eat. Red and green are such vibrant hues that color specialists recommend that they be used sparingly, as accents. Pastel shades of turquoise, blue, or yellow, on the other hand, can create a mood of both contentment and alertness.

Common sense and good taste can usually produce effective blends of colors. Before remodeling or redecorating, however, it might be worthwhile to consult with a color psychologist. It is not enough today to focus on how colors look; we must also be aware of how they affect us.

NEURO-LINGUISTIC PROGRAMMING

In the early 1970s, two Californians, John Grinder and Richard Bandler studied many people they considered to be outstanding communicators. They observed them in person as well as on film and videotape and were able to identify and codify how these people took in sensory impressions, organized them, and came up with a response. Blending their backgrounds of mathematics, Gestalt therapy, and linguistics, Grinder and Bandler developed the basic theories for Neuro-Linguistic Programming (NLP).

Some of NLP's key premises are based on careful observation of other people's nonverbal behavior, such as body, face, and eye movements and breathing patterns. By matching and mirroring other people's behavior, NLP practitioners establish rapport (which they define as opening oneself to receiving information in the way that it is offered; sensing as well as thinking about the other person). People who use NLP adjust both their physical movements and their language to match the other person's communication style.

As evidenced by the number of books and articles that have been written about NLP, more and more people have studied and/or used NLP principles.[12] The process has become a favorite of salespeople and therapists and professionals in many fields. NLP has its critics and skeptics, however, at least in part because of the way people can be manipulated without their knowledge. Laborde attempts to answer that charge in her book, *Influencing with Integrity.* She writes:

> "Now for the difference between influence and manipulation. The distinction is simple. Once you know how to clarify your own desires...you can use the same techniques to clarify the outcomes of any other party involved in the communication. Achieving that party's outcome while you achieve your own is what I call influencing with integrity.
> "Achieving your own outcome at the expense of or even without regard for the other party constitutes manipulation."[13]

It's doubtful that this "I'm doing this for your own good" approach will be enough to satisfy the critics. Nevertheless, librarians who are interested in improving their communication skills should be aware of the basics of NLP, should study them and try them out, and then make up their own minds about NLP's usefulness and validity.

SUMMARY

Our success as communicators is not measured in a general way but by how well we speak, read, write, listen, and think. These skills are all interrelated and equally important. Moreover, they can all be improved with caring and effort.

NOTES

1. John Dewey, *How We Think,* 2d ed. (Boston: D.C. Heath and Company, 1933), pp. 3–6.

2. Edward De Bono, *New Think* (New York: Avon Books, 1971).

3. Roger von Oech, *A Whack on the Side of the Head* (New York: Warner Books, 1983).

4. Jacquelyn Wonder and Priscilla Donavan, *Whole Brain Thinking: Working from Both Sides of the Brain to Achieve Peak Job Performance* (New York: William Morrow and Company, Inc., 1984), pp. 9–10.

5. Dee Joy Coulter, unpublished course material for The Neurology of Learning, April 1979.

6. Karl Albrecht, "Newest Challenge for Trainers: Teaching Trainees How to Think," *Training* 18 (3) (March 1981): 37–44.

7. Richard W. Dodge, "What to Report," *Westinghouse Engineer* (July–September 1962).

8. "The Power of Vocals and Nonverbals in HRD," *Training* 13 (8) (August 1976): 3.

9. Albert Mehrabian, *Public Places and Private Spaces: The Psychology of Work, Play and Living Environments,* (New York: Basic Books, 1976), p. 166.

10. Julian Lamar Veatch, Jr. "Library Architecture and Environmental Design: The Application of Selected Environmental Design Factors to the Planning of Public Library Facilities" (Ph.D. diss., Florida State University, 1979).

11. Dorothee L. Mella, *Color Power: Your Personal Energy Resource* (Albuquerque, NM: Domel Artbooks, 1981), p. 5.

12. Among the many references are R. Bandler and J. Grinder, *The Structure of Magic I: A Book About Language and Therapy* (Palo Alto, CA: Science and Behavior Books, 1975); R. Bandler and J. Grinder, *Frogs Into Princes* (Moab, UT: Real People Press, 1979); L. Cameron-Bandler, *They Lived Happily Ever After: A Book About Achieving Happy Endings in Coupling* (Cupertino, CA: Meta Publications, 1978); and Daniel Goleman, "People Who Read People," *Psychology Today* 13 (2) (July 1979): pp. 66–78.

13. Genie Z. Laborde, *Influencing with Integrity* (Palo Alto,CA: Syntony Publishing, 1984), p. xvii.

Chapter 6
Small-Group Communication

Much of the communication of any organization must, of necessity, take place in small groups. Depending upon past experience with "group work," reactions to a meeting notice may range from "Oh good! Now we can get that problem solved" to "Oh no! Not another meeting."

Organizations vary greatly in the value they place on collective discussions, and, therefore, in the frequency and length of their meetings. Some organizations rarely meet, preferring that decisions be made by individuals and passed along the hierarchy; for these organizations, the staff picnic may be one of the few times they get together. At the other extreme are those organizations that like to meet at the drop of a hat. Group decision making and consensus testing are the norm. Most organizations, including libraries, seem to fall between these extremes and schedule meetings for a variety of purposes, some on a regular and some on an as-needed basis.

Meetings do seem to be essential to effective organizations. Whether they are anticipated or suffered through depends, of course, on many factors. Much of the criticism leveled against group discussions stems from a lack of understanding of crucial group forces and the complexities of leadership. Both training and experience are necessary to turn a collection of people into a group. Some naive managers (perhaps because they themselves have never had the satisfying experience of being part of a fully functioning group) think all they have to do to have a successful meeting is to gather people together.

This chapter will focus on group development phases, group characteristics and forces, small group leadership, highlights of group process, and how to make the most of meetings. Of course, the emphasis will be upon the role of, as well as the impact upon, communication in all of these aspects.

HOW GROUPS DEVELOP

Just as with individuals, small groups—particularly those that are ongoing and meet regularly over time—go through a development process on their way to maturity and fulfillment. Just as with individuals, small groups start out being dependent on authority and do some floundering around while they try to figure out where they're going and how they're going to get there. While working out their task and interpersonal structures and methods, people in groups have a tendency to become frustrated at the time it takes to get going and with other group members who refuse to agree or go along. Frustration leads to conflict. If the group avoids the conflict, its path to maturity will be longer; if the group learns how to resolve the conflict and moves through it, there almost always is a new burst of energy, along with renewed good feeling about both the task and the other group members. Most members of committees or task forces have experienced these typical, and mostly predictable, stages of development.

Scholars in the field of group communication have conducted many studies to determine how groups form and develop. Depending upon the group purpose (whether it is training, therapy, or problem solving) and the length of the group's life, researchers have identified different development stages.[1] John E. Jones identifies four stages or sequential periods of development and separates personal relations and task functions into different tracks.

Stage	Personal Relations	Task Functions
1	Dependency	Orientation
2	Conflict	Organization
3	Cohesion	Data-flow
4	Interdependence	Problem-solving[2]

The use of "task functions" is fairly universal, but what Jones calls "personal relations" has been identified by others as "maintenance functions," "socioemotional functions," "group structure," and the like. Blake and Mouton describe the two dimensions as "concern for task," and "concern for people."[3]

Jones makes the point that group leaders and members, if they are to monitor and influence the development of their groups, should be able to determine the stages of development and what options for growth are available at any given stage. He feels that group development stages are not only predictable, but they can be controlled.[4] The notion that groups can control or even alter their development stages should come as welcome news to those group leaders who have repeatedly watched their groups march through the same predictable stages, feeling that patience until the group finally broke through to maturity was their only recourse.

In new groups, most communication is apt to be task-related. Yet in the group's early stages, the maintenance or people needs require more attention than the task. The getting-acquainted period is vital to later development and should not be hurried unless, of course, the group's purpose involves a crisis situation or inflexible deadline.

When people join new groups, they inevitably engage in mostly self-centered behavior, reflecting their individual concerns. As the concern for self declines, members will gradually pay more attention to each other, wanting to know who the other people are, where they stand on group issues, and how all the individuals are going to interrelate. It is only after the self-oriented and curiosity-about-others phases have been at least partially satisfied that the group can comfortably get down to work.

Task-oriented leaders try to cut short this initial "chitchat" period, failing to recognize that personal interactions on a variety of subjects build a foundation of understanding and cohesiveness. In the later stages of group development, provided that maintenance needs have been met along the way, groups can communicate almost entirely about the task with little or no attention to the socioemotional ramifications.

GROUP CHARACTERISTICS AND FORCES

Several important group characteristics and forces exist that help determine how (and even whether) a group develops.

Goals

When considering the aspects that make up a group's personality, one must be the group's goals. Successful groups make their goals explicit and make sure that group members are committed to them, and that, as much as possible, group goals are meshed with individual goals.

Some groups make the mistake of dispensing with the discussion of goals after the first meeting. But goals do not necessarily stay the same. They need to be discussed regularly and continually reexamined and reevaluated. Perhaps commitment to initial goals has waned. Perhaps over time individual perceptions of the goals have altered. Perhaps situations have changed. All of these possibilities lead to the clear need for communication about goals as an ongoing part of the group process.

Sometimes a group can succeed only after recognizing that the goal they started out with no longer works or is no longer relevant. For instance, a couple's group, when first formed, was built around reading aloud from Dickens, and only Dickens. As such, the group did not flourish; attendance was sporadic. The librarian who furnished them with reading material wisely helped them see that reading aloud was a means to their real goal, which was the opportunity to get together regularly and socialize. Both interest and membership increased when the group began to emphasize the social aspects of their meetings, while at the same time expanding the reading list to include a variety of authors.

Continuity

Another force operating in the group is its continuity or the relative stability of the group's membership. If the membership is continually changing, forces for integration and orientation must be satisfied before genuine task accomplishment can even be launched. The problem is that the addition or subtraction of even one individual significantly changes the group and makes it necessary for the initial stages of group development (what Bormann called the shakedown cruise phase[5]) to begin all over again.

A continual dilemma arises from the issue of whether groups should back up their discussion each time a new or formerly absent member joins the group. Can groups afford the time it takes to communicate past activities and decisions? Can groups afford not to take the time? A partial solution is to ask one of the group members to communicate with the absent or new member before the meeting, to summarize what the person has missed. Thus, no time is taken away from the meeting. But it is only a partial solution because the summary will inevitably be only one person's version of what happened and can cover very little of all the dynamics of what was communicated in a group meeting.

Cohesiveness

A group becomes cohesive when it has achieved a satisfactory blending of forces which bind the members together. Cohesion results from a positive socioemotional climate in which members receive satisfaction from being in the group, feel a degree of closeness and warmth toward each other, and have a sense of pride about being in the group.

One task force in a large public library that was charged with the difficult assignment of developing a policy for collecting entrance and use fees from suburban patrons struggled with the problem for several months. During this process, the group grew so cohesive that they didn't want to disband. It finally became obvious that the policy had been completed and their task was done, but the group was stretching out the details of implementation in order to continue meeting. A wise library director found another assignment so that the group's maturity and cohesiveness could be put to another good use.

Norms

Norms are standards or codes, explicit or implicit, that are accepted by the group members, that guide and regulate thinking and behavior. Norms evolve during the life of the group, largely from the way group members develop their communication patterns. For instance, certain aspects of the group are discussed, then repeated at the next meeting and it becomes a norm for that item to be on the agenda. Such a norm may then be formalized into a policy or unwritten rule. Sometimes implicit and explicit norms are contradictory. For example, there may be an explicit group norm that everyone should speak openly and freely, yet there may also be an implicit norm that certain powerful people in the group are not to be contradicted or challenged.

Norms not only provide useful shortcuts to decisions; they also provide clues to appropriate behavior and often save us the trouble of having to look at the evidence each time we make a decision. For example, people who have developed the norm of meeting at a regular time and place don't have to check with each other about the time and place of the next meeting. Similarly, group members who have developed a procedure of taking turns being chairperson don't have to waste time and energy jockeying for position or competing for status. Norms can be helpful time-savers. On the other hand, a group that insists on blind adherence to its norms because "we've always done it this way" may have an unhealthy attitude. Such a group may find itself meeting out of habit rather than need.

Interestingly enough, those norms that emerge implicitly from the interaction of the group itself and which have not been identified or labeled as norms are often quickly changed when someone points out that a norm has developed. For example, if group members have developed the habit of apologizing or explaining whenever they arrive late, and someone identifies this practice, future apologies may be withheld. It's as if the communication about a norm exposes it as a secret ritual, which because it has been exposed, now has to be changed.

A library staff group developed a norm that each meeting would begin with a "show-and-tell" period in which each person would describe what had occurred in his/her department since the previous meeting. At first, this worked well as a means of communicating and keeping each other informed. But gradually, the show-and-tell period expanded to the point that there was little time left for the items on the agenda. What had begun as a positive norm evolved into a negative one from overuse.

Role Differentiation

To be successful, a group needs a variety of functions or roles performed. Individuals will assume a certain function at a certain time not only because the group needs it at that time but also because there are needs operating within the individual. The most fundamental type of role differentiation occurs between task functions (getting the group's job done) and socioemotional functions (helping members maintain the group and get satisfaction out of how the job is being done).

In most groups, individual members begin to recognize when certain functions are needed, and, although they freely exchange roles, may become associated with special functions. More role specialization occurs in mature groups which recognize that it is more efficient if the primary tasks are shared, if efforts are not duplicated, and if they do not compete for roles. Mature groups allow people to fall into the roles/activities that they are comfortable doing and that they do well. For instance, John may be an excellent summarizer, so the group gradually begins expecting that John will be the one to come up with summaries when they are needed. Julia may have a delightful sense of humor, so the group begins looking to Julia to come up with the right quip or anecdote to relieve tension when the going gets rough.

Of course, there is a danger that groups can become too dependent on the specialists and that group members might lose their flexibility in performing a variety of roles. We remember one group, for instance, in which one member had become expert at keeping the group on track. When that member was absent, the group wandered all over the place without even recognizing that that was what they were doing.

Obviously, role specialization means that communication specialization has occurred because roles are developed and maintained through the group's interaction. Not only what is communicated, but also how and when contribute to the delineation of roles.

Trust

In a group's early stages, the members are usually apprehensive, if not downright fearful, of the uncertainties and the unknown. Signs of mistrust, such as attempts to rely heavily on rules and structure, stiff formality, and unnatural politeness, gradually disappear as trust begins to grow.

One sign of growing trust is a relaxed atmosphere; another is greater acceptance of nonconformity. People begin referring to the group as "we" instead of "you." The gradual building of trust is a key variable in group development.

To the extent that trust develops, group members are able to communicate genuine feelings and perceptions and consistently engage in open and authentic sharing. There are fewer hidden agendas. A valid feedback system can be formed. As trust builds and the group matures, artificial and superficial comments decrease; members no longer worry about maintaining facades. When trust levels are high, communication improves in quantity and quality, resulting in both more cohesiveness and better decision making.

Size

Group size is an important variable because of its effect on both structure and communication. The larger the group, the more structure it demands. Larger groups of approximately 15 or more, for instance, often find two leaders emerging, one who focuses on substance and one who influences procedures. Larger groups need more control and more role specialization. Smaller groups can afford to be more freewheeling.

The more people there are in the group, the less time each individual has to communicate. A group of two has only one relationship, AB, if we can use A and B to identify two individuals. If we add a third person (C) we now have three relationships (AB, AC, and BC). But suddenly the progression takes off so that a group of five has 10 relationships, and a group of 10 has 45 and so on.

GROUP LEADERSHIP

We have already discussed leadership in the broader, organizational sense. Small group leadership, however, calls for a range of special attitudes and skills.

No person is more important to the success of a group session than the one at the top whose job is to gain meaningful response from people. The leader's attitude about people may be far more important than his/her repertoire of skills and techniques. The leader who best serves the group and the larger organization is one who has both a positive attitude about people and their capabilities for group action and the ability to get things done with the help of others.

The leader of a small group meeting has three basic responsibilities that s/he must either assume or delegate to someone else: to (1) guide, (2) stimulate, and (3) control. A leader guides by organizing an agenda and seeing that it is followed, by helping the group proceed clearly from one question or subject to another, by encouraging or making clear transitions and summaries, and by keeping the discussion from straying too far from the subject.

A leader stimulates by creating an atmosphere in which others feel they want to participate. A leader keeps the discussion as interesting and thought-provoking as possible and makes certain that all have the opportunity to participate by gently inviting silent or less vocal members to join in, by raising appropriate and clear questions, and by making sure that all available data are presented.

A leader controls the meeting by seeing to it that the purpose of the session is accomplished. This is done by moving the discussion along from a subject the group would rather stay with. It may be necessary to move toward the evaluative stage of the proposed solutions before the members have exhausted the identification of all possible solutions. Finally, the leader must do all these things with tact and finesse, being careful not to dominate the discussion on the one hand or be too permissive and let the interaction wander aimlessly on the other.

The leader also needs to make sure that both task functions (such as initiating, clarifying, recording, and summarizing) and maintenance functions (such as encouraging, supporting, mediating, and gatekeeping) are being performed. Keeping track of the substance of the discussion and overseeing the process through which the group is moving are twin leadership roles.

Stimulating commitment to the group is also an important function. One way to do this is to guarantee that each member perceives a reason for his/her presence. There must be something in it for the members, and they must have a sense they are needed and that their presence or absence makes a difference.

Leaders need to listen carefully to group members both in and out of meetings in order to discover their goals and attitudes. Equally important, the very act of listening demonstrates that someone cares. Everyone needs a sympathetic audience. When people find someone who cares enough to listen, they can scarcely escape involvement in the group.

Leaders should not fall into the trap of commenting after every contribution made in a session because this stops free-flowing interaction. Members can unwittingly cause this to occur by posing questions of the leader instead of the group as a whole. When the leader prefers not to answer a question, s/he can either turn it back to the person who asked it or redirect the question to the group.

One reason for lack of commitment to a task or group is that people perceive that nothing seems to happen as a result of the meeting. People discuss, make proposals, offer solutions to problems, and then everyone goes away and nothing more is said. Perhaps the problem was poor listening—suggestions and solutions might not have been grasped. Perhaps there was no recording or inadequate recording of the outcomes, so people forgot what had been agreed to; or perhaps no one took the initiative to solidify agreements by summarizing or identifying the times the group reached consensus. Whatever the reason, a definite leadership function is following through. Make certain the group knows what it decided and what it accomplished at the end of each session. These points should be communicated orally as part of the meetings and followed up in writing if there was more than one agenda item. Good leaders do not leave next steps to chance. They make sure all group members receive a progress report and a clear idea of what the next meeting will be about. Even groups that meet only once need a wrap-up or summary at the end so that the members have a feeling of closure and accomplishment.

The final leadership function to be discussed is the important matter of providing for group evaluation and growth. One of the most effective ways to improve group discussions is to build in opportunities and make plans for systematic evaluation. Yet evaluating the group we are a part of is extremely difficult. To do so means stepping outside ourselves as participants and taking on the roles of observer and critic. What's more, groups should not accept everything even an outside evaluator says as absolute truth, particularly if the evaluator is inexperienced or observes the group for only a short time.

It is always valuable for a group to allot time to study its own operations. Many unsuspected problems can be uncovered this way. A means to begin this is to ask each group member to write one word that describes how s/he feels about the group at the moment. The scraps of paper, without identification, are collected, scrambled, and then read aloud. It may come as a surprise to the person who wrote "pleased" or "satisfied" that others are feeling "confused" or "bored." Discussing why people feel certain ways about the group becomes the first step in evaluation.

Too often, however, groups conduct an unstructured, open-ended "How are we doing?" session as their only means of evaluation. Unless the group has developed some criteria against which to judge itself, its analysis is apt to be shallow and unproductive. Having group members evaluate themselves along specific dimensions such as communication skills, ability to deal with conflict, and sharing responsibility for the group's welfare is an effective evaluative process. Individual self- evaluations can then be compared with feedback from others so that goals for improvement can be outlined. (It is best that feedback relate to behavior rather than personality.)

"How can our group communication be improved?" is a question every group should be seriously and continually concerned about. If a group experience creates feelings of frustration, disappointment, or anger, we have a responsibility not only to make our feelings known but also, and more important, to motivate other group members to work together in diagnosing and curing whatever ails the group.

GROUP PROCESS

How groups go about their business, make decisions, and solve problems make up its process, which can be tracked in order to determine such aspects as patterns and amounts of participation and who performs the leadership functions. It is often very useful to have someone observe the group in action and report on the specifics of the group's communication. Problem areas such as uneven participation (overtalkers perhaps monopolizing the discussion) or the failure to come to closure on a specific issue can be identified so that the group can improve the ways in which it operates. Many group members are so involved in making statements and listening to the conversation flow that they fail to notice what is happening in the group process as a whole. Those who do pay attention to the group's process often evolve as the group's informal, if not formal, leaders.

Decision-making and problem-solving discussions are at once the most common and the most difficult to deal with. They are common because to make a decision or solve a problem is often the very reason for the group's existence. They are difficult because the process, to be successful, is inevitably complex. What's more, the process is more time-consuming than for an individual to decide or solve a problem alone. True, two or more heads are better because they contain more information, evidence, and experience than individual heads do. But the process of sharing that information takes much longer.

GROUP DECISION-MAKING PROCESS

Human decisions seem to be made by either discussion, debate, or default. We inquire and investigate, we argue and challenge each other, and sometimes we avoid making a decision—which is, of course, just as much of a decision as making one.

As group members, we are constantly involved in decision making within ourselves and with the rest of the group, yet the process is seldom something we think about consciously. Whether we are merely deciding when and what to talk about or who to elect to chair a committee, we make many decisions without really being aware of how the decision is made or what effect it has on us. The significance of any decision is determined by the presence of commitment. Commitment is not visible; only the behavior that results is visible. Phony agreements in which no real commitment is made have plagued groups throughout history.

Though decision making is not as complex a process as problem solving, it also has a pattern. First, we become aware that we are at a point of choosing an alternative from a group of possibilities. Next, we examine the alternatives and predict the consequences of choosing each one. Last, we make our selection from among the alternatives—in other words, we make our decision.

Groups make decisions in four ways: by force, by arbitration, by majority vote, or by consensus.

Force

The application of force is usually the result of lack of action or decision by a group. If a decision must be made and the group is unable to make it, someone in higher authority may hand a decision down. Fortunately, this rarely happens, but when it does occur, it is more of a default than a decision by the group.

Arbitration

If the group is hopelessly (and perhaps bitterly) split and if the group members see no way to resolve differences, the group may have to resort to arbitration. When this happens, the group brings in a disinterested third party to make the decision. Labor-management disputes are often turned over to a mediator; if the mediator cannot help the group resolve its differences, the problem is then turned over to an arbitrator. Just as with decisions by force, the decision is made not by the group but by an outside individual.

Majority Vote

Voting is a way of life in a democracy, as is the principle of majority rule. But for small groups, voting may sometimes be more of a hindrance than a help. Parliamentary procedure and voting are necessary for groups that are so large (say 15 or more) that not everyone can speak at will, or for groups whose bylaws require public discussion and recorded votes. In large groups, voting is an efficient decision-making process and also has the virtue of protecting and recording any minority viewpoint.

In small groups, however, votes have a way of solidifying positions and making later modifications difficult. But the most serious indictment against voting is that it turns members of a group into winners and losers. Losers may not feel committed to carrying out a decision they voted against. Voting means a decision has been made by quantity rather than quality, and it does little to resolve differences or change people's minds.

Consensus

Rather than meaning unanimity, as some people think, consensus means a general agreement in which all group members have a hand in shaping the decision and, although the decision might not be perfect, group members feel they can accept it and live with its consequences.

Compromise has the connotation of weakness or giving up at least part of what the person wants. "I will not compromise on my position; my demands are 'nonnegotiable.'" When an honest consensus is arrived at, by contrast, the group product is added to by group members and no one is positioned into having to give up something.

Let's look at how this might work in a group of eight people. Member A suggests a policy that could be formulated to solve the problem under discussion. Member B agrees with most of it but asks the group's permission to change part. Member C wants still another modification, which is partly contradictory to what B wants. Member D proposes a change that accommodates both B and C and also includes an aspect about which D is concerned. Member E persuades the group to delete some troublesome phrases. After more discussion, Member F calls for a restatement and summary of what has been agreed to so far. The attempt at restatement brings out some avenues that Members G and H want clarified and amended. Then the entire group agrees to the statement of policy as amended.

This was a consensus because, by the end of the process, no one remembered or cared who proposed the initial policy statement, and each person added something to the formation of the concept that was adopted. Because the amended policy statement belonged to the group rather than to an individual proponent, no one felt called upon to attack or defend. All could concentrate instead on improving and clarifying. The leader of the group working toward consensus does not call for agreement or disagreement, "yes" or "no" votes, but instead asks something like, "Are there any objections to the policy in its revised form?" If the leader hears objections, more discussion is needed to integrate divergent views. If there are no objections, consensus has been reached.

Making decisions by consensus is more effective but also more difficult than voting. It takes longer and requires sensitivity to both verbal and nonverbal communication. It also requires a sense of timing to know when the right moment to culminate the discussion has occurred. Consensus-seeking works best in small, mature groups whose members understand how the process works.

Too much consensus-seeking can damage a group. An interlibrary committee trying to create a training program on interlibrary cooperation and networking developed an ingrained norm in which the majority continually pressured the minority to go along to achieve consensus. Meetings could not be adjourned until a consensus was reached and so meetings got longer and longer. When the majority continually railroaded decisions over the objections of the minority, the whole group suffered. If the minority viewpoint is stifled so that the group continually makes expedient rather than wise decisions, the result is what Janis called "groupthink."[6]

GROUP PROBLEM-SOLVING PROCESS

Problem solving is considered to be a separate and more complicated process than decision making, yet there is obviously some overlap since problems cannot be solved without making decisions. (In fact, problems often arise because of decisions we make.) And we need to make a variety of decisions along the way to solving a problem.

Groups solve their problems either through the traditional or nontraditional method or a combination. The traditional method owes its origins to John Dewey's description of what he called the "reflective thinking process," the steps people use to effectively solve problems. Dewey distinguished "reflective" from other kinds of thinking by noting it "involves (1) a state of doubt, hesitation, perplexity, mental difficulty...and (2) an act of searching, hunting, inquiring, to find material that will resolve the doubt..."[7]

Most people will recognize the traditional problem-solving method involved in the "scientific method":

1. A problem is identified.
2. Relevant data are gathered.
3. A hypothesis is formulated.
4. The hypothesis is empirically tested.

Although they may not be recognized as Dewey's two phases, these are usually the steps that groups go through to solve their problems (but not necessarily in this order):

Problem formulation
finding and clarifying the elements of the problem
analyzing the problem
reformulating the problem (if necessary)

Problem solution
solution proposals
solution testing
putting the solution into action

Many groups have learned that an additional step between the formulation and the solving of a problem saves time in the long run. That is the setting of criteria or yardsticks by which the effectiveness of alternative solutions can be measured. Typical criteria are (1) feasibility (will the plan work?); (2) practicality (are the means to carry out the plan available?); and (3) ramifications (will this plan create new problems?). The determination of criteria helps decide how the group will know when they have found a really good solution.

Nontraditional problem solvers, on the other hand, avoid using steps and rigid procedures, preferring techniques such as brainstorming and imagining the future without restrictions from the past. They look for gestalt insights and intuitive flashes. They think of metaphors and analogies to picture the problem in different ways.

An effective combination would be to use the logical steps to identify and analyze the problem and the creative approach to brainstorm all possible solutions. Then the group could return to the traditional problem-solving method to evaluate the solutions and select the best one for implementation. Because evaluation and criticism stifle creativity, it often works best to separate the brainstorming and evaluation processes into separate functions, perhaps even performed by separate groups. The "think tank" people create solutions; the administrators decide which ones to implement.

It is impossible for groups to solve problems without communication. We ask questions, make suggestions, present hypotheses, and synthesize the written and oral expressions of many people. Communication is an integral part of the entire process. And, of course, it is possible that communication (its quality or its absence) may be the problem we are working to solve.

CHARACTERISTICS OF GROUP CONTRIBUTIONS

When group members are communicating, their contributions may take the form of questions, statements, or exclamations. Contributions may be long or short; they may have several purposes or just one. Naturally, not all contributions are equally effective. Some move the group forward, others hold it back. Although all of the communication skills previously examined are important in group sessions as well, successful group interactions also require the following.

- Relevance. Just as an individual may find his/her mind wandering into irrelevant channels, groups also go off on tangents. Relevance does not necessarily mean that a contribution must be exactly on the topic. It means that a discussant's statement or question should at least be centered on significant task or interpersonal needs.
- Relatedness. Sometimes a contribution may be relevant to the topic, but it is not related to the comments that have just preceded it. This is like dumping parts of a watch on the table. Each one is relevant, to be sure, but useless until put together. Unless comments are related to what other people

have said, the discussion cannot develop a theme or arrive at a conclusion.

- Timing. Good ideas are sometimes lost in group discussion because they were presented prematurely, before the group was ready, or too late, after the group had moved past the point of relevance.
- Clarity. Group members should not assume shared meanings but check for understanding. If terms are not defined and rephrased continually, group members may find out they have not been talking about the same things.
- Appropriate length. Contributions made in a group should be of sufficient length to make the point but not so long that they deprive other group members of equal access. An interesting phenomenon of group life is that the larger the group, the longer the speeches. It's as if each person is fearful that s/he will not have the floor again and should, therefore, filibuster.

Making the Most of Meetings

Clearly, the organizational meeting, which is basically a pooling of information, knowledge, facts, opinions, feelings, and judgments, is well-suited to serve a number of important purposes. Typical purposes are decision making, problem solving, transferring information, and training. Committee and staff meetings are ideal for these purposes because they provide opportunities for questions, discussion, feedback, and clarification. If interaction is not needed or desired, don't hold a meeting. Write a memo instead.

Just because meetings are important and used extensively doesn't guarantee that they are always effective. We all hear complaints about the frustration caused by meetings which are badly organized and poorly conducted and, therefore, totally useless. You do not have to attend many meetings like this to conclude that your library is holding too many meetings or the leaders do not know how to use a meeting effectively.

Meetings which waste time may even have had as their original purpose the saving of time. What goes wrong? It could be that the director rushes into the meeting with everything planned (probably too much for one meeting) and opens the meeting with an apology for having called it. She promises the group the meeting will end promptly at a given time because she knows several people have other meetings and appointments at that time; in fact, she too has to attend another meeting following this one. Everything about her has communicated haste. Maybe she glances at her watch when someone begins to speak, or when a discussion develops, cuts it off with a reminder that time is passing and there are still many items to be "covered."

The group member who interrupts this steamrolling affair to ask a question or contribute information is a brave and possibly fool-hardy person. Members quickly learn that speed is more important than getting the work done effectively or making the best possible decision. The leader may go through the motions of discussing the items on the agenda and asking questions which no one feels free to explore; no real communication takes place. Participation is stifled by the compulsive drive to cover the agenda and to do so in the specified time. Such a meeting is a waste of everyone's time and should never have been called.

Another kind of useless meeting is the one in which the leader uses the meeting to conceal his/her decision. Having already made up their minds, these leaders pretend that the meeting has been called to discuss the problem and arrive at a solution. As a rule, it does not take long for group members to catch on that their primary function in such a meeting is to act as a rubber stamp and that the meeting is a sham.

Planning Improves Effectiveness

One of the first considerations to confront is the question of the need for the meeting. Is it really necessary to meet or would a memo or phone call or quick conversation be better? Sometimes a few minutes spent with each person separately is more effective and productive than a meeting. Nothing destroys the effectiveness of meetings like the overuse of them. But when meetings are necessary, how should they be prepared for? All of the following suggestions serve the function of clarifying communication and expectations as well as ensuring that everyone gets the key messages involved before, during, and after the meeting.

1. Determine the purpose of the meeting and communicate it to the participants so that they will have realistic expecta- tions and will know how to prepare. Everyone should have a clear idea of what the meeting is intended to achieve and how they will know if it was a success or failure.
2. Decide who should participate. Select only those people who have a need to be involved and who are able to contribute to the purpose of the group. The value of a committee or staff meeting is lessened if too many people are involved. Between four and eight participants is generally considered ideal for decision making; groups of nine to 12 will work if the group has matured; anything over 12 means that members cannot speak as often or as long as they would like and the time required to hear from everyone greatly expands.

3. Prepare the agenda. An effective agenda not only contains a list of the subjects to be covered but also in what sequence; about how much time is expected to be devoted to each; and which items are for information only, which are for discussion and which are for decision making. Properly drawn, the agenda has the power of shortening and clarifying a meeting. Ideally, group members should be encouraged to suggest additional or substitute agenda items of their own either before or during the meeting.

4. Arrange the best time to meet. Timing is important because of the difficulties of meshing the calendars of busy people; allowing enough time for full discussion is also a key.

5. Arrange the best place to meet. Many factors enter into this decision. If the meeting is ritualistic, use the most impressive conference room you have or arrange for an appropriate room somewhere in the community. On the other hand, it is better to avoid the office of a high status member if you are holding a decision-making meeting because this kind of room may inhibit the free flow of communication required. In choosing the meeting place, select one that is compatible for your purpose. For example, a very effective meeting may occur as a kind of huddle in the back room or even standing in the hall, when the purpose is clear and the task can be completed in a few minutes. In general, choose a small, simple meeting room with few distractions where the members can sit close enough together to see and hear each other easily.

6. Arrange for someone to record minutes or decisions. Often passed around as an onerous job, keeping track of decisions and discussion themes is a crucial means of providing a sense of accomplishment when copies of the minutes or documentation arrive; in addition, the group minutes are the impetus to follow through with who is to do what next. The group recorder should ask for a few minutes at the end of the meeting in order to check out his/her perceptions with the group as a whole. Otherwise, the minutes should be headed, "One person's version of what we discussed and decided," and time should be set aside at the next meeting to amend or ratify the recorder's notes.

HANDLING PARTICIPATION

During the course of any meeting, groups are likely to have to deal with the people who represent the two extremes of participation—the overtalker and the undertalker. Both types of behavior can be troublesome to a group, but we don't know how best to handle the situation unless we know the reasons behind the behavior. We include this problem under the discussion of meeting management rather than under the section on leadership because participation is a group problem and, as such, is better handled by the group than by the elected or appointed leader. A fellow group member can more easily encourage or discourage the undertalkers and overtalkers than the leader. Of course, group members have to be aware of the problem and be willing to help deal with it.

Rarely is it appropriate to cut off the person who talks too much, although it is tempting when frustration mounts and other methods have failed. Really listening, fairly and without prejudice, to such a person will often help locate his/her need and give you a clue as to how to help the overtalker become effective in the group. Perhaps this person needs recognition; perhaps s/he does not feel listened to or appreciated. Another strategy is to ask the overtalker's help in bringing out the quiet group members.

How best to handle the undertalker is equally perplexing. Almost every manual on conducting meetings stresses the importance of securing full participation from all members because groups need all of their resources. The assumption is that if a member participates, s/he will look more favorably upon the decision, be more inclined to feel that it is his/her own, and then do what is expected to implement it. Some of the current research has found, however, that the more important measure of members' satisfaction with a meeting is the extent to which they feel free to participate. The group's goal, then, is more realistic if it is to create a climate in which everyone feels free to talk and not one where everyone *must* talk. Groups should not, therefore, strive for equal participation but for equal opportunity to participate.

But how can we create such a climate? Asking questions is a good approach. You may point out to the group that some have not had the opportunity to participate. Say something like, "Several of us have had a great deal of input on this matter, but there are some who have not had an opportunity to talk. Is there anyone else with ideas to share?" Avoid putting the undertalker on the spot by calling on him/her. Ask for opinions or feelings, giving advance warning that you want to hear from everyone on this point. Start with the more vocal and move around to the less vocal last.

ADVANTAGES OF SUCCESSFUL GROUP COMMUNICATION

The values of successful group communication can be summarized as five advantages:

1. It establishes teamwork. Full and effective group communication can develop a fine spirit of teamwork by creating a high degree of interest among the people involved.

2. It develops pride in the group and in the organization. Since people have the chance to express their ideas, viewpoints, and opinions, both individual and group morale are improved. Free exchange of ideas shows that each person is a real part of the organization and is considered to have something worthwhile to contribute.

3. It generates new ideas. By its very nature, group communication demands active participation both in listening and speaking. In well-run groups, ideas are infectious and lead to other, better ideas.

4. It provides satisfaction through problem solving and accomplishment. All group members benefit from seeing their solutions carried out and knowing they contributed to a successful outcome.

5. It offers training in leadership. Group meetings are an ideal place for the development of self-confidence and the ability to think about problems analytically. What's more, learning to share leadership and responsibility for a group's progress and welfare provides a training ground for similar activities in the larger, parent organization.

WHEN A COLLECTION OF PEOPLE BECOMES A REAL GROUP

A meeting consists of a group of people which becomes an entity with a style and personality of its own. Each participant brings with him or her a personality, values, feelings and needs. Yet when people combine in a meeting, they become something more than the sum total of the individual members. As each person influences the others and, in turn, is influenced by them, a synergy develops. The collection of people has indeed become a group.

What are the signs that you have developed a cohesive, mature group? Here are some: People come early to meetings and are seldom absent. They obviously enjoy the task and each other. They listen to each other. They share responsibility for the group, often putting the welfare of the group ahead of their own needs. They manage conflict constructively and do not feel the need to compete for roles or status. They laugh and have fun. They volunteer for tasks and follow through without prompting.

Sound too good to be true? It may be an impossible dream to develop all those qualities in the same group. But it is a dream worth pursuing.

NOTES

1. See, for example, B. W. Tuckman, "Developmental Sequence in Small Groups," *Psychological Bulletin* 63 (1965) 384–99, and Warren Bennis, "Patterns and Vicissitudes in T-Group Development," in *T-Group Theory and Laboratory Method,* ed. by Leland P. Bradford, Jack R. Gibb, and Kenneth D. Benne (New York: John Wiley & Sons, Inc., 1964), pp. 248–78.

2. John E. Jones, "A Model of Group Development," in J. William Pfeiffer and John E. Jones, *The 1973 Annual Handbook for Group Facilitators.* La Jolla, CA: University Associates, Inc., 1973, p. 129.

3. Robert R. Blake and Jane S. Mouton, *The Managerial Grid* (Houston, TX: Gulf Publishing Co., 1964).

4. Jones, p. 127.

5. Ernest G. Bormann, *Discussion and Group Methods: Theory and Practice,* 2d ed. (New York: Harper & Row, Publishers, 1975), pp. 220–24.

6. Irving L. Janis, "Groupthink," *Psychology Today,* 5 (1971), p. 43.

7. John Dewey, *How We Think* (Boston: D. C. Heath & Company, 1933), p. 12.

Part III
Communication and Change

Introduction

Every library faces some kind of change today. Some are relocating to new buildings, some have new administrators or management teams, and some are shifting to automation. At the same time that they struggle with the difficulties of change, librarians also face exciting new possibilities. Change cannot only allow them to do their present tasks better, but it also offers new functions, services, and tools that can accomplish their work more quickly and accurately. Although changing times present dilemmas and personal frustrations, they also offer splendid opportunities.

Effective interpersonal and organizational communication are crucial for changing libraries. As librarians deal with a wide range of technological and attitudinal upheaval, communication is the key that enables changes to be planned and put in place, and, once in place, to then make them work. That is the focus of this section of the book. Chapter 7, "Understanding the Change Process," deals with the overall process and prospect of change. It describes the major changes ahead for librarians, including those related to new electronic capabilities and some of the effects these changes will probably have on libraries' organizational communication. Chapter 8, "Communication Strategies for Changing Libraries," offers specific strategies to help librarians prepare for and cope with change and to develop the flexibility to welcome change in a positive way.

Chapter 7
Understanding the Change Process

We all deal with change continually; nothing stays the same. Whether we feel buffeted by change, while futilely trying to hang on to the status quo, or whether we rush headlong into the new and the strange, we know that change is a given in our lives. We all know, intellectually, that without change and growth, we and our organizations will become stagnant and nonfunctional. Emotionally, however, our response may be less accepting. What we fail to realize is that all of our decisions and plans are steps toward the future which either promote or impede change. Thus, it is important for us to see ourselves as designers of change, not as victims. John Schaar said it this way:

> "The future is not a result of choices among alternative paths offered by the present, but a place that is created— created first in mind and will, created next in activity. The future is not some place we are going to, but one we are creating. The paths to it are not found but made, and the activity of making them changes both the maker and the destination."[1]

But what exactly do we mean by change? Admitting that the definition is an elusive one, Kanter describes change as involving "the crystallization of new action possibilities (new policies, new behaviors, new patterns, new methodologies, new products, or new market ideas) based on reconceptualized patterns in the organization."[2] Two keys here should be emphasized: (1) crystallizing new action possibilities and (2) reconceptualizing patterns. The first refers to deliberate strategies and the second underscores the need for new perceptions and new ways of thinking.

Thus, librarians must combine new concepts and action. Ideally, individuals and libraries acknowledge the need for change, envision the future they want, then strategically devise not only how to survive, but how to effectively grow. In reality, however, the rate and complexity of change often seem to outrun the ability to predict or control it.

PLANNING FOR CHANGE

Planned change is an adaptive process consisting of a series of decisions, actions, and responses intended to improve the organization. In response to a crisis situation, decisions and actions are often haphazard, effective only in the short term. A more rational approach involves preparing a plan that anticipates the future and includes decisions that give clear organizational direction. Basically, planning is an effort to guide change by reducing its risks and uncertainties and increasing its probabilities of success.

During the last quarter of a century, Organizational Development (OD) has emerged as a process to guide organizations as they determine and implement needed change. OD is defined by Beckhard as a "planned, organization-wide effort managed from the top, to increase organizational effectiveness and health through deliberate interventions in the organization's 'processes,' using behavioral-science knowledge to develop and perpetuate change. A prime emphasis of its practitioners and techniques is that of the importance of information and communication."[3] An OD practitioner can help an organization to analyze its present structure and functions, envision its future, make decisions for change, and then put those changes into action. Each of these steps requires effective organizational communication. For, especially during times of change, the need for information is critical.

Many planning models address this need. Reflecting the general trend, library literature increasingly features books and articles on library planning. Two recent examples are these: (1) the Public Library Association's Planning Process emphasizes collecting information, working with groups internally and externally, and using strong lines of communication. Most of the processes concentrate on the flow of information to and from decision makers; and (2) the Management Review and Analysis Program developed by the Association of Research Libraries stresses the importance of internal communication for planning, development, and evaluation.

BASIC CHANGE MODELS

Models are useful to illustrate basic concepts for those who work in and are responsible for libraries undergoing change. A simple, one-dimensional view of change, developed by Kurt Lewin,[4] is shown in Figure 11. The solid line A represents the status quo, which is kept in place by the balance of driving and resisting forces pushing against each other. Driving forces, which are pressures pushing in a particular direction, seek to initiate movement and keep it going. Resisting forces work against that direction and seek to maintain the current balance. The forces vary in their strength and persistence. If driving forces become stronger and/or resisting forces weaken, Line A will move toward the lesser pressure to a new balance point, Line B. Change occurs when the new balance is established. The change *process* is what altered the forces and caused the new balance to come about.

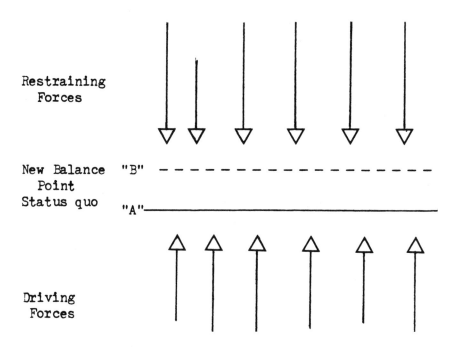

Figure 11. Lewin's Force Field Model.

For example, the director of a library decides to automate circulation. Some driving forces that would support the change would be an overworked circulation staff, the need for more accurate records, and the report of good results by another library that had recently automated circulation. Some restraining forces could be the present staff fearing that their competency is not up to the change, the expense of an automated process, and a lack of solid information on the best system for the library's situation. These forces, in balance, would tend to maintain the status quo. However, an unexpected financial donation or a change in staff opinion could radically alter the circumstances and tip the balance—creating change.

Lewin describes change as occurring in three sequential stages: (1) An imbalance of forces "unfreezes" the status quo; (2) movement continues until a new state of equilibrium is reached; and (3) when the new equilibrium is stabilized and maintained, a new pattern "freezes." Thus, the status quo changes and the new pattern is instituted. Although oversimplified, this model presents a picture of personal as well as organizational change. More sophisticated models of change essentially build from this early concept.

Havelock and Havelock identify several patterns of organizational change. Each is a process with a primary function.

1. Change as a problem-solving process. The need is felt and articulated as a problem, followed by a search for solutions and resources. Then the best solution is selected, based on such criteria as its workability and its acceptance by those affected and those who are to implement it. Planning for the change and implementing it follow.

2. Change as a research-development and diffusion process. A rational sequence of change is assumed that includes research, development, and packaging prior to its mass dissemination to accepting recipients. It involves a long time period, high initial development cost, and division of labor.

3. Change as a process of social interaction. This pattern emphasizes how change diffuses through a social system, affecting and being affected by networks of social relations, interpersonal contacts, and group membership.

After describing these, Havelock and Havelock bring them together in a composite model:

4. Change as a linkage process. Beginning with a felt need to solve a problem, a diagnosis is made leading to searching for a solution and applying it. But this pattern emphasizes a reciprocal and meaningful relationship with outside resources. This relationship, in turn, develops into a social influence network that links internal and external elements. This broadens the impact of the change and deepens its effects.[5]

Similarly, Rogers and Shoemaker also picture how innovations or changes diffuse through an organization, whether the decision to adopt them is made as a personal option, a collective choice, or dictated by an authority. Four functions are required of this diffusion process: (1) knowledge (exposure to the innovation's existence), (2) persuasion (formation of a favorable or unfavorable attitude toward it), (3) decision (action taken that leads to a choice to adopt or reject), and (4) confirmation (acceptance or rejection of the decision made).[6] Rogers and Shoemaker also describe five steps for the adoption of innovative ideas as (1) awareness, (2) interest, (3) evaluation, (4) trial, and (5) adoption.[7]

On a more specific level, Vincent E. Giuliano, with Arthur D. Little, Inc., makes a strong case for the need for intense human communication and interaction during in-depth organizational change. Change, he says, is possible only when information is communicated in such a way that the individual will, at some point, accept and act upon it and not just hear what is being communicated without really listening to it. He suggests that when little change is required, information transfer can be one-way and noninteractive. For example, a memo might merely direct: "The Circulation Unit staff will use form C18 instead of C14 to report daily circulation statistics."

Moderate present change or the prospect of significant future change, on the other hand, requires interaction (two-way communication and active feedback) between the information source and its user. An example would be when a unit head or supervisor explains a new scheduling pattern or on-the-job training requirements using one-to-one dialog or a meeting allowing discussion.

When fundamental personal or organizational change is required, however, individual and organizational behavior must be changed; this often colors people's attitudes toward that change. Thus, strong and intense human interaction is necessary, Giuliano maintains, to effect change. Consequently, libraries engaged in major change can anticipate that communication must be a powerful factor in their change effort.[8]

Change models such as these result from our efforts to understand change and our hopes to control it. Note that each model has pictured change as a process over time rather than as a one-time event. And note also that each has acknowledged the importance of information and communication within that process.

CHANGE AGENTS

Change is not an impersonal process. People work to make it happen; people work to resist it. Active supporters of change, termed "change agents," work in their own ways to make change possible. Some will work from within the library, others from outside. Personal gain or organizational advantages may be motives. However, no matter the motives, their efforts work for change.

Rogers and Shoemaker identify five types of personalities in terms of how they adopt change.

1. "Innovators" make up two-and-a-half percent of the population. These venturesome individuals often can afford to change, having little investment in old ways.
2. "Early adopters" are respectable individuals, open to information and usually concerned with the esteem of colleagues. Comprising 13½ percent of the population, they often hold the key to the diffusion of innovations.
3. The "early majority" consist of 34 percent and are important links in the diffusion process. They are deliberate types, reflective, and interact with their peers.

4. The "late majority" are skeptical, persuaded primarily by peer pressure or job requirements to make the change. They comprise 34 percent of the population.

5. The "laggards," which make up 16 percent of the total, are suspicious of change and those who try to bring it about, and they will do whatever they can to forestall it.[9]

Individuals described in these personality categories vary according to the change contemplated. An innovator in one area might be a laggard in another. Innovators and early adopters are proponents of change—the change agents. Late adopters and laggards resist change; early majority people can swing the tide for change and late majority people can delay it.

Havelock and Havelock expand on four specific leadership roles[10] that change agents play in an organization undergoing planned change.

- The catalyst challenges the status quo, prompting the organization to see its problems and commit effort and resources to resolving them. A catalyst is important to initiate the move out of inertia and then, from time to time, to renew that focus, spurring the problem-solving process, advocating change.
- The solution giver gives answers, chooses among alternatives, and channels ideas to solve problems. Often seen as the authority, this role can dominate the process, blocking others from being involved, and investing themselves in the process.
- The process helper aids the overall sequence of events by defining needs, setting objectives, discovering resources, selecting and adopting solutions, and then evaluating the results. Those in this role know how to accomplish change by supporting the various processes that must be done, tending to ensure the continuity and direction of planned change.
- The resource linker matches needs with resources such as information, funds, staff, and outside perspective. Needs must be identified and resources discovered and used throughout the process of change.

We could wish that each of these roles were available to us in times of change. In reality, we are fortunate if at least some members of our organization have forward-looking approaches and assume some of these roles. Sometimes, of course, a change agent may be capable of assuming more than one role.

RESISTANCE TO CHANGE

Resistance, like support, is made up of attitudes and behaviors. These may be overt and clearly seen, or covert. Resistance to change may translate into resistance to the planning process or, more personally, to change agents themselves. Thus, it could completely stall a library trying to move toward change.

Although blind resistance to change is not desirable since it thwarts needed change, thoughtful resistance can be valid and valuable. First, considered resistance provides a creative energy and reasoned perspective to balance forces moving too rapidly toward change. Without it, chaos reigns. Second, this kind of considered resistance, like the devil's advocate role, can bring forth useful information for planning and implementing change. The presence of a devil's advocate style means that the group cannot get away with superficial thinking about the change but must adequately defend its position.

A major reason for resistance to change is that for some people, maybe most people, change takes a physical and psychological toll. Change affects people profoundly, especially when they have strong personal investments in existing methods, situations, or relationships. Resistance under these conditions can certainly be understood.

Resistance may be based on opinions people have formed as a result of the information they have about the change. Resistance can also be expected if the nature of the change is unclear or ambiguous, especially to those who will be affected by it. Vagueness increases fear of the unknown and the unpredictable, heightening the sense that people lack control in the situation. Disseminating convincing and complete information about the proposed change may be enough to alter opinions and, therefore, resistance. But when individual beliefs or values are the basis for resistance, more than simple information is required because beliefs and values change slowly, if at all.

Ironically, library managers, as organizational leaders, are charged with providing the driving force for needed change; yet at the same time they are responsible for preserving the organization's stability. Thus, by virtue of their positions, library directors must be driving and resisting forces at the same time. Both individual staff members and library managers, as change supporters and resisters, have valid roles to play in changing libraries. Each force influences balance and movement toward or away from change.

PRINCIPAL CHANGES AHEAD FOR LIBRARIES

From the vantage point of the 1980s, it is obviously impossible to predict all of the changes that will confront the library world in the years to come. We have therefore chosen what we consider to be four major trends of the future. Our focus will be on how these trends will affect libraries in general and their organizational communication in particular.

Trend Number One: Changing to the Age of Information

Historians as well as futurists like Toffler and Naisbitt agree that the U.S. is shifting away from the agricultural and industrial eras and entering the Age of Information. This change is predicted to be more profound and far-reaching than all of the previous shifts put together. Increasing numbers of jobs and even new occupations, as well as entire industries, are now devoted to the generation and manipulation of information.

Librarians, like people in every other profession, find themselves right in the middle of this trend. But unlike other professions, librarians, as the traditional keepers and dispensers of information, would logically be expected to be in the forefront, not left behind.

Perhaps because libraries as a whole have been slow to respond instead of leading the way, many new organizations are now expressing their eagerness to serve society's information needs and are actively competing to do so. Their messages are slick and sophisticated: "We are in the information business" and "We are your source for knowing." Where libraries have formerly kept low profiles, with understated, if any, self-promotion, they now must gear up to meet the challenge or lose their position in the marketplace.

How will librarians handle the problems inherent in an economy based on information (instead of agriculture or industry)? Will libraries be able to keep up with the needs for ever-expanding storage capacity along with the demand for faster (some say instant) retrieval? What will be the library's role in dealing with information pollution, the increase in the pornographic, the violent and the tasteless, let alone the completely inaccurate, that is an inevitable part of opening more and more doors to more and more communication? True, the library stores and dispenses information rather than creating it, and librarians have sought to avoid censorship. Nevertheless, personal and professional choices made by today's and tomorrow's librarians will undoubtedly influence the classification and evaluation of information as worthy, relevant, and/or useful. Will librarians serve as increasingly important links between unrestrained information on the one hand and encouraging the public to help determine information accuracy and relevance on the other?

The effectiveness of the almost unlimited information capacity of modern communication systems slows at the bottleneck of how much the individual can assimilate it. New means for summarizing and cross referencing will have to keep pace with the technology. Will librarians spend more time abstracting and interpreting information?

Perhaps it will be a librarian who figures out a way to classify all human ideas into a manageable, usable system.

Futurist Theobald affirms the central and vital role that libraries will play in the Age of Information:

> "The library's function will be more vital in the information and communications world now developing than it has ever been before. Linking people with data and facts, trends and patterns, ideas and myths is our primary need if we are to move successfully through the [societal] transformation now gathering speed so rapidly."[11]

Trend Number Two: Changing from Manual to Automated Operations

Just as with the fields of banking and education and most business and industry today, the use of electronic technology is increasing in libraries. Some libraries are moving rapidly to incorporate new information technology; others are more tentative. A few are still ignoring the trend. According to Matthews and Associates, Inc., well over 600 turnkey automated library systems have been installed, and the number is steadily increasing.[12] As a result, most library personnel working today, sometime in their careers, will work in and with libraries that have incorporated electronic technology or those in the process of doing so. Preparing for this certain outcome is important for personnel at all levels, but especially for library managers.

Academic, government, industrial, and research libraries are in the forefront of the change to automation. They stand to gain the most from being able to communicate with other libraries because they have overlapping interests and often require speedy response. They are also most likely to be close to or within organizations that have and use computers, paving the way for them to automate the library. For the most part, public and school libraries are moving more slowly, the large ones preceding the smaller.

Internally, the more extensively technologies are incorporated, the more profound are the effects upon the library's organizational structure and how it communicates. Modified lines of authority, span of control, and decision making will result. New points for sending and receiving information can knit formerly dispersed and isolated functions, special skills, and work locations. Thus, when appropriately connected, library staff can become more individually effective and can jointly focus on organizational goals.

Externally, strong communication links can (1) serve users' informational needs directly, (2) share resources with other libraries, and (3) sustain the library's position in the information marketplace. Serving users' informational needs—the basic business of the library—can be tremendously expanded using automated processes.

With skilled use, a computer can provide access to the library's catalog or other bibliographic resources with unmatched speed and accuracy. (One concomitant problem is that newer bibliographical tools are offered with electronic access only, thus becoming increasingly unavailable to manual search.) Computer links allow cooperating libraries to quickly tap information about each other's holdings for reference, interlibrary loan, or collection development. These activities were formerly done by meeting, mail, or telephone. Finally, electronic capabilities enable the library to offer competitive services in the information marketplace, much of which is being initiated on the basis of automation.

One of the major impacts of increasing electronic and other technologies is that on the library building itself and how space is utilized. A library that now has 15 drawers of on-order files estimates that they will only need 15 disks when their microcomputer is installed. At the same time, user access to the library's collection will increase. Picture the space now required by the New York Public Library's card catalog in order to list its holdings (88 miles of book stacks). Then imagine the difference when a computer terminal two feet square can indicate all holdings plus whether it is available and what alternative selections exist.

Lancaster sees automation as "...a powerful force operating on the library as a whole, bringing predictable and unpredictable changes in the nature of processes, and implying a reconsideration of all our traditional ideas on how the library should be run and how work should be allocated."[13] Thus, today's librarians face changes in day-to-day operations as well as the library's basic functions.

Resistance to Automation

Despite the fact (or maybe because of it) that major shifts to automation appear to be inevitable, change of this kind does not come easily to any library. Since technological capabilities usually precede institutional and personal adaptations, it is the rare library that can accomplish a smooth, successful conversion to automation. Resistance to automation may be rooted not only in the general reasons for resistance to change already discussed but also in a common perception that the new technologies are cold, impersonal, and alien. The computer's languages and techniques are foreign. That, together with its mystique as being scientific, error-proof, and difficult to master, reinforces barriers to acceptance.

Not only do individuals perceive new technologies as changing their tasks, routines, position, status, and power, but they also see them as threatening to their jobs. Some employees see themselves as inferior to such machines or see the machine intruding between them and their tasks, including their interaction with their coworkers and library users. They see their formal and informal work groups and networks disrupted. Requirements for new skills, changes in the approach to library services, and revised performance appraisal criteria all add to the unease caused by introducing computers into libraries. Though the reasons are many, they often result in suspicion and resistance to automation.

Are these fears groundless? University of California librarian Joe Rosenthal is quoted as saying that automation has not caused a single staff layoff. He says:

> "We have done a lot in the way of shifting jobs and assignments. And, in general, I would say that the caliber and the skills of our staff have increased, developed, and become more complex over the years because of automation and because automation has helped reduce the amount of tedious work."[14]

Even with a clear perspective and knowledge of the advantages to change, library administrators often underestimate the care and patience required to reverse this negative attitude among their staff. The greatest fear throughout the library world is that libraries and librarians will no longer be needed and will therefore disappear. We have dealt with print on paper for 500 years, and the prospect of books and periodicals becoming antiques and museum pieces is "mind boggling." But many people believe that books will be around for a long time. As Boulder (CO) Public Library Director Marcelee Gralapp expressed it, "Books are not going to be replaced; they are still the best means of preserving information. But our job is to provide information in the best form available. For some purposes, disks and audio and video tapes may be better."

Stueart also believes that librarians have a future. He maintains:

> "Professionals working in libraries will be negotiators, identifying needs; facilitators, providing effective search strategies; educators, familiar with the literature in all of its formats; and information brokers, providing current awareness services for the populations they serve. The library's role will be one of integrating the information environment.[15]

Many, including Lancaster, who look ahead more than a decade, envision the library less as a building than as a dynamic information and communication center, offering integrated access to information available from many different sources. Competent information workers help patrons use the materials and technologies of the library. Or, they, themselves may produce the information required by the patron. Down the road, people skills are still required in the library, although the structure as we know it may not be.

Stueart and Lancaster both urge that a distinction be made between the library and the librarian. They think the importance of the library will diminish because of lack of function while the librarian will persist because of essential information- and people-handling skills. Lee R. McLaughlin, chief of the U.S. Air Force Academy

Library Acquisitions Division at Colorado Springs (CO), recently added a personal dimension to this point of view by saying, "Machines can't think of alternatives the way trained people can. The major difference I see ahead is that computers will change the way we get the work out."

Although they may change in character and function, libraries will continue to be the guardians of our culture and heritage and will continue to be used for self-education and personal improvement. Many people believe that libraries, particularly public libraries, are our best evidence and practice of the American democracy's precept of free access to information. First-rate libraries enable us to know where our civilization has been and get an indication of where it is going.

Trend Number Three: Changing Patterns of Library Usage and Service

Each library, as it attempts to reflect and attract the values and interests of its clientele, has its own way of anticipating user needs and its own methods to attract people to use the library and its services. Patterns of library use reflect national trends and local issues. They also reflect the effectiveness of local libraries' messages that promote their innovative information services (from local area information and referral to computer-assisted database searches) and their special materials collections (from rare books to audiovisual materials to toys and sculpture). None of this, of course, is remarkably new. But, the emphasis on effective library marketing techniques and the increased awareness of how vital marketing is to libraries is new.

Although most library usage surveys indicate that book use continues to represent the reading public's major interest, libraries are not the only source of books. Thus, marketing libraries solely on the basis of books—the traditional stock in trade—is likely to be short-sighted. Promoting the more general information services must take into account library users who have their own computers and can reach directly to any number of information networks from the Library of Congress to the local electronic bulletin board. Yet the increasing numbers of American functional illiterates and the declining numbers of young readers must also be considered. This does not necessarily mean that the library's clientele is shrinking. Rather it means that the library may be working with different clientele and providing different services. For example, a school or public library may respond to society's concern about illiteracy by developing a literacy learning center for nonreaders. Or an automated university library may refocus its assistance to users to increase their ability to use automated searching and reference services.

Effective marketing—including clear internal and external communication—explains library changes by providing usage facts and trends. Internally, library staff must see and accept the challenge, then work for change. Externally, the library's message must be clear and direct so the public realizes the need for and scope of change. Effective communication using electronic or traditional methods can create new perceptions about the library or alter existing ones. The primary pressures on librarians now are to quickly read the needs of the clientele and respond to them, understand the nature of the information sector competition, and clearly communicate the library's message to staff and clientele.

Trend Number Four: The Changing Library Work Force

In Chapter 3, "Special Concerns of Library Managers," we identified three worker ethics—traditional, challenge, and lifestyle. As our cultural values shift, American workers will naturally reflect and represent the new values. There are fewer traditional work ethic people today and more work challenge and lifestyle workers. Perhaps because of our nation's volatile economy during the last few decades, increasing numbers of workers at all ages appear to be more security-minded.

Another factor affecting the library work force is the mobility of people in our society, which causes costly turnover. For instance, in most two-career families, career-focused women are likely to move for good work opportunities; yet it is still the norm that the husband's career path is the major reason for family moves. But since more women than men have chosen librarianship as their career, library managers must deal with the probability that they will lose many of their female staff. Thus, managers often find themselves investing in training staff that will ultimately be of primary benefit to some other library.

Like other employers, libraries must make constant adjustments so that job placement, work assignments and methods of supervision mesh the skills of the available work force with the work to be done. When dynamic economic, societal, and labor force changes are compounded by internal library change, the pressures on library managers to be good communicators are intensified.

IMPACT OF CHANGES ON ORGANIZATIONAL COMMUNICATION

Obviously, shifts in organizational structure, personnel responsibilities, or even location that result from the changes we have been discussing inevitably alter communication patterns as well as work flow. An effective, well-established organizational communication system can provide the glue that holds the organization together during transition and change.

For the most part, the impact of changes on the library's organizational communication depends on two significant factors: (1) capability and (2) attitude. Changes can expand current capabilities and attitudes or cut them back, thus modifying their patterns or direction. For example, relocation may increase communication with some parts of the community and decrease communication with other sections. Or a new management team or organizational restructuring may open vertical communication channels to increase information flowing upwards. Even though the capability to direct information upwards increases in a newly restructured library organization, individuals must make choices whether or not to use that capability. Such choices are based on individual perceptions and attitudes.

The most extensive change in the volume and dimensions of organizational communication is likely to be from automating library functions. With technological advances, information capability is increased tremendously for individual workers as well as for the entire library organization. Let us examine more closely how capability and attitudinal factors relate to the impact of major change such as automation on organizational communication.

The computer can collect, store, and reassemble information in massive quantities. Its programs are a major communication achievement, as they enable humans to manipulate information in multiple, simultaneous ways. Information can thus be translated into decisions and actions more quickly than ever before. Thus, this new technology enables libraries to handle expanded quantities and new forms of information with far less time and labor. For example, incredible amounts of circulation and acquisition information can be handled with speed and accuracy. This information can then be redesigned in a number of different ways and distributed to various people for review or decision. Library administrative, reference, and public relations staffs can use these improved communication capabilities both within the library and externally.

The technological capability already exists to carry out these functions. Nonetheless, even these new technological capabilities still depend on human capabilities such as skill and judgment to make decisions as what to communicate, to whom, and when and how to do that. The need for human communication is not replaced in the electronic library nor is less understanding or skill required. Rather, the dimensions of human communication are expanded even as the character and method of communication change. Humans, not machines, must determine the desired patterns for the flow and use of information.

Given technological and human capabilities, the library organization itself must be able to support and sustain both humans and technology. Also, the library must have capabilities for decision making, coordination, and cooperation. Technological, human, and organizational capabilities are major factors in changing libraries. But skilled personnel given access to computer terminals, basic files, and programs in a supportive organization still require another essential ingredient: the willingness to use these capabilities. Translating the capabilities into individual behavior that will apply them depends on the attitude of individuals because people decide if, when, and how to use the capabilities.

An example of how capabilities and attitudes must work together in a typical automated function can be seen in relation to electronic mail. Electronic mail allows individuals to deliver messages from one point to another in the form of memos, reports, or personal messages, which may be printed or displayed on a terminal screen. For example, a simple message from an acquisitions librarian to a subject specialist may report the current status of materials on order. Or a manager's memo might incorporate information from stored files, such as current budget figures; add a new policy statement; and be sent to all relevant staff members with terminal access—all in a few moments. Electronic mail is fast, does not interrupt work flow, coordinates scheduled projects, eliminates "telephone tag," and provides immediate dissemination and quick response. This mechanized system, however, is not always an effective substitute for face-to-face interaction or telephone dialog.

Yet given the capability for electronic mail, personnel in one extensively automated public library use it rarely, although it has been heavily promoted and available for some time. Reasons cited, such as "I'm just not in the habit," may indicate subtle resistance to its use, even though many other kinds of automation are accepted and used. In contrast, a floor- to-ceiling dry erase panel, or white board, installed near the staff entrance in the same library continues to be heavily used for organizational and personal messages. No one knows for sure whether the use of the white board is more efficient, offers unique advantages, or is just a hard habit to replace.

Communication plays a key role in developing the capability and in forming the attitudes that change libraries. And since the changes are on an organizational scale, the communication must also be viewed from an organizational perspective. Three major organizational aspects will be most affected by change. They are (1) communication channels, (2) relationships, and (3) power and influence.

Communication Channels

In the traditional library, people, paper, and telephones are the major means of internal communication. For the most part, information is delivered via one-to-one conversations, group meetings, memos, documents, and bulletin boards. In the electronic library, these methods are not so much displaced as enhanced by new possibilities.

For example, from dispersed work sites, staff can compile, update, store, and move internal information rapidly throughout the system. When needed, information can be called for at any location and displayed on a screen or printed. Word processing, a writing and editing tool, can quickly and flexibly blend reports and forms to create "original" documents or correspondence from existing files. Multiple files or documents can be combined, reformatted, and reorganized, then replicated and disseminated.

Use of computerized internal communication methods carries at least two important implications. First, greater dependence upon the written word requires more care to ensure clarity and understanding and to lessen semantic difficulties and unintended meanings. Written communication tends to be more "information dense," that is, more packed with meaning than is the spoken word. Written communication skill becomes even more vital, and not all staff members possess this skill. Misunderstandings may be more widespread and have more serious consequences because the instant feedback of face-to-face communication is not available.

Second, use of electronic communication relies heavily on individual initiative, which may be dampened when the computer's capability does not meet expectations, when access to terminals is difficult, or when the method is discounted or unused by others. What's more, skill is impaired if instruction or training is not available or is ineffective.

Further, in the automated library, many procedures are formalized more precisely than in nonautomated libraries in order to meet technological needs. An example and a symbol of this is the extensive written documentation required to describe what the user, the program, and the computer are to do and how they must do it. Documentation provides an invaluable record for day-to-day operating decisions for those responsible for working with the computer, as well as a base to work out "bugs." Usually written by staff responsible for developing the program, documentation describes the routine in jargon, programing language, and technical notes. To make this information usable for others, it is usually translated into manuals written for the layperson.

Electronic mail as described earlier is an example of a new communication channel. Teleconferencing is another. Teleconferencing is an electronic mechanism which enables two or more people at different locations to "conference" with one another via messages sent on terminals or by live television or telephone transmission. This method can provide an economic alternative to travel for meetings and continuing education.

New communication channels such as cable television can be used, with very positive results, to inform the public of the library's role and range of services. However, careful thought must go into these messages so that the progressive nature of the "new" library is balanced by the valued "old" traditions of service and personal attention. The image created must be realistic so that it builds expectations that can indeed be met. If users get the impression that promised improvements will hinder rather than help them get the information and services they want, they may look elsewhere for their information needs.

In libraries undergoing change not involving electronic technology, communication channels are also modified, though less dramatically. Assigning new responsibilities brings new personal communication styles into play. Introducing changed management principles also puts a new organizational communication style in place. Changing libraries often alter their means as well as their style of communicating. One of the major indicators that a library is undergoing change is that it communicates differently.

Relationships

Relationships are also altered in changing libraries. Relationships between people and work units evolve from their physical proximity, organizational position, involvement in shared or linked tasks, and friendships based on common values and personal feelings. Relationships, whether work-related or personal, are complex, dynamic, and not fully predictable. But the common denominator of all relationships is their dependence upon communication.

When jobs are changed and space is rearranged, old relationships are bound to be affected. For example, work sites in a new library may be more physically isolated, or those in an electronic library may be separated by structural barriers and by the individual's required focus and concentration on the computer. These factors alter interpersonal exchanges. Those who work at terminals may feel they have to distance themselves from informal interchange. Those involved in the automated functions might be seen, by management, by themselves, and by others, as separate from traditional library functions, related only at points where traditional and automated aspects meet directly. Traditional supervisory relationships may change if those supervised have substantially greater technical knowledge about their function than the supervisor.

A system staff—that is, those responsible for technical computer functions—must build communication bridges between automated and nonautomated library functions and the different staff groups involved. Systems staff, whether developed in-house or brought in from outside, become a central part of the library, altering communication patterns and old relationships.

The threat to valued and stable relationships is at the root of much of the resistance to change. Change often means upsetting existing relationships, including those of power and influence.

Power and Influence

Another result of changing organizational structure, job design, and communication channels is a shift in power and influence. In fact, restructuring is often done deliberately to build new power bases. These may simply designate new formal authority and positions or devise more complex informal influence centers. Generally speaking, those individuals with access to key information and the ability to use new channels will tend to elevate their status and increase the power they actually possess and that they are perceived by others to have.

A 1980 study by Bjorn-Anderson and Rasmussen identified power shifts as one of the primary effects of automation. People found themselves either higher or lower in the organizational hierarchy. Levels at which decision making takes place change, as do the overall manner and degree to which power is exercised. Following automation, functional roles of nonmanagerial employees were more standardized, formalized, and specialized. In addition, workers found they had to plan more in advance, had far less freedom to determine their own work methods, and tended to communicate more impersonally.[16]

COMMUNICATION AND CHANGE

Because communication is so closely interwoven with other elements in a changing library and because each library's situation is unique, all of the effects of change on the library's organizational communication will be difficult to isolate and assess—or to predict safely. Change agents and planners, however, can almost certainly anticipate two important results from instituting change.

1. Change will lead to an increased awareness of organizational communication as a whole, as well as its importance to all levels of employees. This is a significant and frequent by-product of change, especially when the change is extensive, such as in the case of relocation, reorganization, or automation. Individually, staff members may be better able to anticipate their own need to communicate because of the change process. As they focus on the information they need, planners may examine the library's organizational communication for the first time. This, in turn, can lead to instituting improved methods of communication within the library.

2. As a result of this new awareness, planners and managers can design new communication patterns to accommodate the changes and move specific information to specific places. These intentional new patterns will be based on a conscious

awareness of (a) the need to exchange information; (b) what types of messages are needed; and (c) the formal and informal channels to do so. Often, such patterns are more effective than the earlier ones formed by tradition, time, and personalities.

Change of any kind, particularly that which takes place in the course of automating the library, inevitably will involve growing pains, setbacks, and miscalculations. Effective organizational communication, together with planning, can help in successfully managing change. When these elements are effective, good information, careful decision making, and prepared personnel are the result. During times of change, communication can facilitate, guide, and limit change, as well as help to integrate individual needs and organizational goals within the dynamic situation. Strategic communication can motivate personnel not only to accommodate to change but also to become positively involved in helping to bring it about.

NOTES

1. John Schaar, quoted in *Inventing the Future: Participatory Planning Process for Alternative Futures,* by Gerald C. Hanberry (College Park, MD: University of Maryland University College, 1975), p. 12.

2. Rosabeth Moss Kanter, *The Change Masters* (New York: Simon and Schuster, 1983), p. 279.

3. Richard Beckhard, *Organization Development: Strategies and Models* (Reading, MA: Addison-Wesley Publishing, 1969), p. 9.

4. Edgar H. Schein, "The Mechanisms of Change," in *The Planning of Change,* ed. Warren G. Bennis, Kenneth D. Benne, and Robert Chin, 2d ed. (New York: Holt, Rinehart and Winston, Inc., 1969), pp. 98–107.

5. Ronald G. Havelock and Mary C. Havelock, *Training for Change Agents* (Ann Arbor, MI: Institute for Social Research, 1973), pp. 7–38.

6. Everett M. Rogers and F. Floyd Shoemaker, *Communication of Innovations: A Cross-Cultural Approach* (New York: Free Press, 1971), p. 25.

7. Rogers and Shoemaker, pp. 22–23.

8. Vincent E. Giuliano, "Communication Levels Involved in Change," in *Readings in Interpersonal and Organizational Communication* ed. Richard C. Huseman et al. (Boston: Holbrook Press, Inc. 1969), pp. 17–202.

9. Rogers and Shoemaker, pp. 174–96.

10. Havelock and Havelock, pp. 60–63.

11. Robert Theobald, "The Future of the Librarian," *Public Libraries* 20 (3) (Fall 1981): 74–76.

12. Figures compiled by Joe Matthews, Matthews and Associates, Inc., Grass Valley, CA., consultants in automated systems for libraries.

13. Wilfrid F. Lancaster, ed. *The Role of the Library in an Electronic Society. Proceedings of the 1979 Clinic on Library Applications of Data Processing* (Urbana-Champaign, IL: University of Illinois, Graduate School of Library Science, 1980), p. 52.

14. Russell Schoch, "Checking Out the Library," *California Monthly* (March–April, 1984): 15–17.

15. Robert D. Stueart, "Libraries: A New Role" in *Books, Libraries and Electronics: Essays on the Future of Written Communication,* by Efrem Sigel (White Plains, NY: Knowledge Industry Publications, 1982), pp. 114–15.

16. Neils Bjorn-Anderson and Leif Bloch Rasmussen, "Sociological Implications of Computer Systems," in *Human Interaction with Computers,* ed. H. T. Smith and T. R. G. Green (New York: Academic Press, 1980).

Chapter 8
Communication Strategies for Changing Libraries

Planned communication strategies to initiate and sustain change can ease the impact of change on people and the library. Such strategies are needed at all levels—administrative, supervisory, and staff—to enable interdepartmental information to flow throughout the organization effectively. Each change strategy must anticipate the kind and amount of information people will require and be flexible enough to respond to dynamic situations.

This chapter offers a range of communication strategies librarians can use to introduce, initiate, implement, and integrate change. These are ideas, not prescriptions, a composite from experiences of others facing similar situations.

Basic guidelines for planning and personnel offer a foundation for developing communication strategy. Schein describes four conditions essential for an organization to cope successfully with a rapidly changing environment. These conditions provide useful precepts to keep in mind while designing communication strategies. Implicitly and explicitly, they acknowledge communication as:

> "1. ... the ability to take in and communicate information reliably and validly. 2. ... internal flexibility and creativity to make the changes which are demanded by the information obtained. 3. ... integration and commitment to the goals of the organization, from which come the willingness to change. 4. ... an internal climate of support and freedom from threat, since being threatened undermines good communication, reduces flexibility, and stimulates self-protection rather than concern for the total system."[1]

PLANNING GUIDELINES

Planning for change is vital. Incorporate organization communication planning to support your plans for change.

1. Design communication strategies to "fit" the library's existing communication patterns, management style, and decision- making process. Use transitional patterns that build bridges from the old to the new situation.

2. Combine varied communication approaches (one-way and two-way patterns, formal and informal, one-to-one and group, oral and printed) so that everyone is as clearly and fully informed as possible about the changes to be made. Ensure that channels foster and sustain two-way communication by encouraging feedback, dialog, networking and assessment. Integrate present communication channels with new ones. Consider conditions such as timing and management objectives.

3. Explore alternative means of bringing about desired change, such as conducting a demonstration project, holding special training events, purchasing new equipment, or bringing in an outside consultant.

4. Identify communication methods and resources available for use in the change effort.

5. Document your planning process to provide an organizational history of decisions and actions and to preserve the integrity of library direction and history despite staff turnover.

PERSONNEL GUIDELINES

Personnel are the library's prime communicators inside and outside the library. Therefore:

1. Take into account their specialized expertise in placing personnel and assigning responsibilities. Consider their communication and interpersonal skills and their expectations as well as work roles and technical skills.

2. Ensure that key personnel communicate extensively and in-depth, particularly if the change is significant.

3. Provide strong social interaction components to help offset the "hi-tech" emphasis and impact of automation.

4. Ensure that all departments and services have equal access to information.

5. Increase the availability of top and middle managers as sources of information, reassurance, and feedback for staff members.
6. Decrease temporarily the degree of staff accountability for results when new skills are being mastered or change has disrupted normal working conditions.
7. Identify and use the motivations and incentives likely to influence people to accept changes.
8. Identify supportive and resisting forces and individuals involved. Assess their strength and influence and analyze their communication styles.
9. Make special efforts to build communication bridges among the library staff, professional and paraprofessional, and the systems staff.
10. Develop communication policies and procedure manuals to guide personnel.

In addition to these general guidelines, more specific strategies should be considered. The term "strategy" is not used here to infer an adversarial position. Rather, strategy conveys the sense of a carefully thought-out plan or method designed to accomplish a given goal. Overall, strategies are usually a coordinated series of actions guided by deliberate intent and direction. Their success (i.e., appropriateness and effectiveness) depends a great deal upon the circumstances involved.

STRATEGIES FOR ANALYSIS AND PLANNING

Before any contemplated changes—a new building, reorganized library functions, or automation—can take place, make a detailed study to look at the problems the changes are intended to remedy. The possibilities include having an outside consultant examine the situation, gathering relevant statistics and analyzing existing problems, or holding meetings to collect opinions and perspectives. Analysis and study of available opinions and facts can refine the definition of the situation and explore alternative approaches to solve it.

Establishing and maintaining effective communication channels during this stage is critical. Personnel are essential information sources and their cooperation and acceptance is needed. If personnel are "protected" from information about the prospect of change, anxiety and insecurity may result when the information eventually leaks out. One possible consequence is that individuals resisting change may deliberately withhold or distort information needed for analysis.

If the change contemplated involves automation, a formal systems analysis is required. This organized, step-by-step process analyzes programs, procedures, problems, and information flow. Systems analysts examine the library in terms of potential automation, identifying its present information patterns first. Their major information sources are organizational documents (forms, minutes, manuals, charts), observation, and interviews. To design automation to accommodate present and future needs, they audit the structure, processes, storage, and transmission of information, then look at the work force, the physical facilities, timing, control—even the norms—as well as the overall work flow. At this point, they make a presentation which identifies why and where the present system is inadequate and what should be done. Then, in proposing automated library functions and means of communication, their proposal focuses to a great extent on what information is needed by whom, where it must come from, and how it can be transmitted.

Typically, system analysts and system staff have strong analytic and technical skills. Often, however, library personnel see systems people as causing the "trouble" change makes. Required rules and protocols are resented and seen as disruptive to the creative thinking and judgment of librarians. In part at least, this attitude may be rooted in communication problems that come about because systems jargon and librarian jargon differ. Establishing communication links between the two groups early in the transitional process can encourage acceptance and understanding of change. At this stage, overall communication strategies are planned to:

- elicit information needed for the analysis
- temper feelings of anxiety
- provide credible information to curtail rumors
- overcome distance and lack of understanding between library personnel and systems people
- initiate the process of involving personnel in the changes to come.

Important specific strategies for analysis and planning might include these:

- Involve key personnel in analyzing problem areas and in reaching decisions about change to increase their understanding and chances of acceptance and support.
- Share the rationale behind the analysis and planning. Emphasize how changes may solve critical library problems. Identify who will make key decisions and when. Spell out the criteria on which decisions will be made.
- Be clear about the benefits for individuals as well as for the library as a whole. Balance these with a realistic picture of difficulties and problems that can be anticipated.
- Hold frequent staff briefings to demonstrate sincere openness to feedback as well as to give progress reports.
- Show how the dominant values and traditions of the library are related to analysis and planning efforts.

- Explore how supportive the climate for change is by response to the analysis and planning effort.
- Make timetables public and realistic. Be aware that frequent delays and rescheduling will raise a credibility question and lower initial levels of interest and enthusiasm.
- Inform the library's governance bodies, staff, and clientele and sound out their initial support for analysis and planning. Note initial responses as tips to resources and points of support and resistance.

The importance of this initial stage cannot be overemphasized. This is the first point for "unfreezing" (as discussed in Chapter 7, "Understanding the Change Process") and the point where individual "turf" is first threatened. The major issue is how to turn this stage from one that solidifies resistance to one that opens individuals to the possibilities of change.

STRATEGIES TO INTRODUCE THE IDEA OF CHANGE

Reactions to the prospect of change vary widely. Three factors influence reactions. One is the nature of the change: What does it concern? How does it affect me? A second is the scope of the change: How will my world be altered? The third is the state of our personal world: stable, insecure, or up and down. Some will react to the idea of change by feeling threatened and fearful, others will feel heightened interest and energy, and still others will respond with passive resignation. Effective strategies to introduce any major change must address the full range of these potential reactions.

How each person perceives change is important since staff must act collectively to effectively implement it. Acceptance of change is far more likely when individuals perceive future possibilities as being beneficial to them and as exciting rather than threatening. If, on the other hand, people see themselves as powerless or in jeopardy, resistance will be strong. Starting on the "wrong foot" can create persistent resistance, seriously impairing the likelihood of future successful change. Effective communication, particularly at this time, will help shape individual perceptions and attitudes.

General overall strategies during this stage focus on preparing the way for firm rather than exploratory planning and development by (1) building a general climate of acceptance of the need for change, (2) revealing a realistic picture of long- and short-range changes, (3) helping individuals relate themselves to the change and perceive its benefits, and (4) involving personnel in creating and influencing change.

More specific strategies to introduce the idea of change might include these:

- Involve personnel, especially department heads and supervisors, in planning for the change. These key positions link management and staff and, as such, can be facilitators of change. Supervisors who are in tune with staff attitude and morale can help build staff understanding of the importance and benefits of the prospective changes and can pass along to management operational problems or concerns (real or perceived) identified by staff.
- Identify key supporters of the change and discover the reasons for their support. Elicit their questions and concerns and respond to them. Channel information through their networks to spread understanding and strengthen support throughout the organization.
- Identify key resisters and discover their rationale for opposing the change. Address their questions and fears in an open and frank manner to increase credibility. Deal directly with feelings of uncertainty and risk. Elicit feedback.
- Provide additional information for key supporters and/or resisters by arranging for visits to other, similar libraries that made successful changeovers, participating in job exchanges, having speakers at staff meetings, and attending professional conferences.
- Communicate decisions, once made, throughout the library; also supply the major supporting evidence and backup information.
- Update personnel regularly on progress made and timetables set for introducing changes.
- Inform staff about the goals of the change, the ability of the change to remedy library problems, the consequences if change is not adopted, the advantages of the change, and how the change fits in with the library's mission. These statements must be realistic and not include promises that, if unfulfilled, will impair the effort's credibility.
- Assure staff of continued two-way exchanges of information, questions, and observations. These exchanges can diffuse new ideas, increase chances for their acceptance, and adapt them for a realistic fit.
- Help individuals see themselves as part of the change, integrated with other staff and work units into a total library effort.
- Integrate systems staff into the library's formal and informal networks to make use of their expertise, increase mutual understanding, and exchange ideas.
- Explain and demonstrate the incentives and rewards for sharing and disseminating information in contrast to retaining it. These may require new or changed policies (such as "perks") and forms (such as performance appraisals) and may need to

be backed up with opportunities to improve staff skills in communicating, networking, and information handling.

In addition to these strategies, consider using a transition task force or team. This planning, coordinating, and communicating change agent group can be responsible for designing and managing each stage. Such a group offers greater energy, expertise, and influence than a single individual or a management group alone. To be effective, its members must be credible, able to spend adequate time, knowledgeable in terms of the task to be done and the process of change, able to support and assist each other, and must be adept at solving problems. For its communication and other responsibilities, this group must be representative of all staff levels, be clear on its information and decision-making authority, and able to disseminate its information skillfully through formal channels and multiple networks. Such a group, if sufficiently open and flexible, can be instrumental in gaining support for change and adapting it to the library. Since committees and transition teams do not operate totally independently, they must take into account the regular decision-making patterns in the library and its present distribution of power and influence as well as the purpose of the transition team itself.

ADDITIONAL STRATEGIES TO DEAL WITH RESISTANCE

Resistance can be expected if the nature of the change is unclear or ambiguous, especially to those directly affected. Vagueness increases fear of the unknown and unpredictable and the sense of losing control. If a change seems significant enough to warrant opposition, resistance will undoubtedly increase. Resistance is often regarded as something to "break down" and get past. However, when individuals or organizations attempt to do this by threat, coercion, persuasion, or reasoning, resisters fight back by "not hearing" or by discounting both the proposed change and the tactics. The result is even more entrenched resistance.

A better approach is to work *with* resistance, using it to provide valuable information. Ask for negative feedback, perhaps with questions such as: "Do you see potential problems with the proposed changes?" Although accepting criticism is often difficult, receiving it as needed information and using it greatly improves the chances that change will be successfully made. This process requires an open and honest climate and assurances that the resister is being listened to and that the feedback is welcomed. Then, if possible, ask the resister what is acceptable or positive about the desired change in order to establish some common ground.

Effective communication in the early stages can forestall many of the typical causes of resistance. Resistance often results from management's failure to anticipate it, or unexpected technical problems that surface, or an inadequate approach to the problems to be solved. Libraries with adequate communication experience fewer of these problems. Dealing with resistance early makes it easier to sail smoothly through initiating, implementing, and institutionalizing desired change.

STRATEGIES TO INITIATE CHANGE

At this stage, the impact of the change cannot be ignored, for it begins to affect organizational structure and jobs. For a change to automation, for example, individuals watch as tasks are reduced to their component parts and procedures are tightly prescribed and paced to fit the computer. Learners tackle the mastery of new skills. Tasks and interaction focus on the computer and its functions rather than on coworkers. Much of what is seen at this stage may confirm the mystique and threat of automation.

Actually initiating change with action steps, such as installing procedures or equipment and adding special systems personnel, reveals that the commitment has been made and the process of change, though it can be altered, is now irrevocable. Now, staff who opted to "wait and see" as well as those who were unaware of plans for automating may experience job stress and exhibit increased resistance. As a result, individuals feeling threatened may be hostile and may reject specific task-related changes or demonstrate deliberate dysfunction, withdrawal, or confrontation.

Overall communication strategies during this stage will be directed to: (1) encourage acceptance of the change by clients as well as personnel, (2) enable staff to understand the changes being put into effect and deal with them in a problem-solving manner and (3) preserve an open stance to learning new techniques and tools. Strategies must take into account the time required (usually longer than anticipated) to enable people to accept new ideas and adapt to them.

Specific communication strategies to initiate change include:

- Update staff on these problems as they arise.
- Design informational, instructional, or promotional communications to deepen staff understanding of changes.
- Open up diverse opportunities for staff participation in change. Assure individuals some control and creativity in relating to the changes.
- Demonstrate the value of the change with a function that illustrates how the new procedure is improved and can benefit workers by making tasks more varied and interesting and, at the same time, bringing better results.
- Elicit staff ideas for ways to use new methods and tools to keep communication lines open and to foster staff involve-

ment. Work out procedures to help staff assess their work with an eye toward improvement.

- Respond to feedback with open communication. Facilitate direct communication, not confrontation, between advocates and resisters of change.
- Initiate changeover to automation with high-interest, all- purpose electronic communication or games to stimulate interest and, to involve people individually and familiarize them with the possibilities technology offers.
- Build public interest and support for the new capabilities by demonstrating the new electronic services. Positive feedback from clientele can strengthen internal support and vice versa.
- Focus staff development opportunities on technological applications and new skill development in such a way that they strengthen organizational communication pathways and develop natural staff networks.
- Provide communication training opportunities for key personnel responsible for instituting changes.
- Construct links between special project or systems staff and regular library work units to prevent isolation and to bridge gaps caused by personnel turnover.
- Encourage good role models who can convey how to overcome initial frustration and move on to use new methods on the job. These people can present positive attitudes and offer enthusiastic support for other staff.

STRATEGIES TO IMPLEMENT CHANGE

Implementing change means that new methods and procedures have been established. At this time early successes and problems surface and must be addressed. How the administration and library staff respond is, as always, crucial. As has been previously noted, extensive organizational change restructures communication patterns and new methods and procedures alter work flow and relationships. Even when alternative formal channels of communication have been planned, they take time to become effective and familiar. The disrupted informal networks also require time for readjustment.

Thus, overall communication strategies at this time are meant to ensure timely information and response to problems found and to help staff and, in some cases clientele, adapt to the new situation.

Communication strategies to implement change include these:

- Structure opportunities for physical mobility and social exchange, especially for those in jobs requiring protracted concentration or isolation.

- Communicate with library users encountering new equipment and approaches. Provide increased staff attention, signage, and special guides and manuals for users. Build in protection against inaccurate referrals by keeping staff knowledgeable on changes underway. Train public service staff, particularly, as informational bridge builders between the clientele and library—this is especially important during the installation of the changes.

- Disseminate current information regularly to sustain the momentum of change. Avoid turning the inevitable malfunctions, obstacles, and difficulties into barriers which can dampen early enthusiasm or build resistance and uncertainty (or perhaps certainty that it won't work!).

- Prevent information overload. Only distribute key, pragmatic information that addresses priority needs.

- Use rituals to herald the coming of the new (such as naming a new computer) and the passing of the old (such as burying outdated files).

- Implement first in areas where the advantages are most needed and results will be quickly evident. Use results to demonstrate benefits resulting from the change. Elicit staff ideas for further applications.

- Supplement training activities with regular follow-up support, including supervision.

- Prevent special project or systems staff from becoming isolated from other library personnel.

- Help staff improve their interpersonal communication accuracy at this time with guidelines, tips, coaching, and training.

- Form a troubleshooting team to resolve implementation problems that emerge and to serve as informal consultants to identify needs and concerns and respond to them.

- Elicit feedback from all staff levels regarding benefits and problems.

At the point of implementation, some staff unhappy with the changes will choose to leave. This may disrupt many communication channels and networks newly put in place. Promptly installing alternative patterns for information exchange should help maintain stability.

STRATEGIES TO INSTITUTIONALIZE CHANGE

Institutionalization of change occurs when the organization's structure, information flow, and internal integrity become more stable and predictable. It is the time Lewin refers to as "re-freezing." At this time, people work smoothly together and their work is coordinated and efficient. Work-related behavior becomes more consistent. Informal networks again communicate the news of the organization and hold morale and support steady. New socialization patterns channel feedback and instructions as well as work issues. Decisions, policies, and structures are finally seen as "normal." Communication strategies reflect this as they stabilize change. With major upheaval past, they reveal new patterns reflecting the commitment throughout the library.

Communication strategies to institutionalize change include:

1. Develop communication channels that maintain the present situation and keep it current. Ensure that information flows up, down, and laterally. Channels could include meetings, retreats, manuals, instructions, and memos.
2. Develop policy statements and procedure manuals that specify formal communication patterns and stress the value and means of information exchange within the organization. Raise the consciousness of all personnel about organizational communication, as well as their roles and responsibilities to make it work.
3. Communicate regularly with the library's staff, clientele, and governance bodies about the results of the changes now in place, particularly those groups affected by the changes.
4. Accommodate staff turnover with orientation and training. Encourage opportunities for new relationships aimed at information exchange. Ease the impact of high turnover by filling information gaps, assuring key technical support, and stabilizing work relationships.

When change is at the point of becoming institutionalized, the library climate will become more relaxed and productive. At last, it is time to reap the benefits of previous efforts, disruptions, and anxieties. If, at each of these stages, communication strategies have been effective, your change efforts will have been relatively smoothly accomplished.

ASSESSING THE EFFECTIVENESS OF COMMUNICATION STRATEGIES

Evaluating the effectiveness of communication strategies should not be delayed until all planned changes are in place. Rather, periodic assessment of progress should be done throughout the process of change. The intent of assessment is not to research but rather to discover the results of what has been done either intentionally or unintentionally and then to improve and adapt, based on the findings.

Assessment can be done on different levels depending on the time available, the level of interest, and the benefits expected from doing it. Two likely areas to explore include (1) how adequate is the library to gather the information it needs and then to communicate it? and (2) what information was most essential to raise interest or decrease resistance to change? Basically, managers will want to know how effective their communication processes are and whether they worked.

Exact measures will be difficult to obtain because communication is so interrelated with other complex and dynamic functions. Beckhard and Harris identify the types of questions any such assessment should address:

1. What organizational variables are of primary concern, such as (a) attitudes toward organizational goals, and morale; (b) organizational processes—communication, decision making, problem solving, and conflict management; (c) organizational structure—clarity of role responsibilities, reward system, and reporting relationships; and (d) organizational outcomes— productivity, sales, and turnover?

2. Who in the system possesses the kinds of information desired?

3. Who will use the information produced?

4. Is there a plan to feed back the data provided to the sources of those data? To the whole organization?"[2]

Thus, the action plan necessary at this point is to define your purpose for the assessment, identify types and sources of information you need, select your methods and timing, allocate resources (including time) for the entire evaluation process, and then implement your action plan.

Some guidelines to keep in mind in relation to these procedures would include:

1. Consider methods such as interviews, questionnaires, observations, organizational records, reporting forms, or outside consultants. Develop specific forms and/or interviews to collect information from selected staff or all personnel.

2. Develop criteria related to the information you seek, such as the degree of support the change has and how satisfied personnel are with information they have received, the attitudes and perceptions workers hold about their jobs and work situations, the relationship of the effectiveness of managerial problem solving and decision making during the changeover period, and the information managers got.

3. Time the assessment after people have had some experience with the changes being made but before their frustration is acute.

4. Report information and results found to those giving the information and to decision makers.

The importance of such assessment can be realized when you look ahead to see the many changes that the future will bring. Learning from each time you initiate and implement change will improve your own skills as a change agent and enable your library to become an adaptive institution in the society.

Changing libraries is exciting and exhausting work. It opens up opportunities for librarians to analyze and evaluate library functions and then develop new patterns of working together. This, in turn, tests present goals, both personal and organizational, and, for managers and supervisors, gives each person unequalled opportunities to improve his/her ability to manage.

Peter Drucker comments, "A time of turbulence is also one of great opportunity for those who can understand, accept, and exploit the new realities. It is above all a time of opportunity for leadership."[3] From times of change come the library's leaders. What is at stake today and tomorrow for those leaders—for libraries and librarians—is far too important to be left to chance.

NOTES

1. Edgar H. Schein, "Organizational Effectiveness," in *Behavioral Decisions in Organizations,* ed. Alvar Elbing (New York: Scott, Foresman and Co., 1970, pp. 767–75).

2. Richard Beckhard and Reuben T. Harris, *Organizational Transitions: Managing Complex Change* (Reading, MA: Addison-Wesley Publishing Co., 1977), p. 89.

3. Peter Drucker, *Managing in Turbulent Times* (New York: Harper & Row, 1980), p. 5.

Selected Bibliography

Abell, Millicent D. "Aspects of Upward Communications in a Public Library." In *Reader in Library Administration*, edited by Paul Wasserman and Mary Lee Bundy, pp. 248–53. Washington, DC: NCR Microcard Editions, 1968.

Albrecht, Karl. "Newest Challenge for Trainers: Teaching Trainees How to Think." *Training* 18 (3) (March 1981): 37–44.

Association of Research Libraries, Office of Management Studies. Systems and Procedures Exchange Center. SPEC Kit 54 Internal Communication: Policies and Procedures. May 1979.

———. SPEC Kit 55 Internal Communication: Staff and Supervisory Roles. June 1979.

———. SPEC Kit 56 External Communication. July–August 1979.

Beckhard, Richard. *Organization Development: Strategies and Models.* Reading, MA: Addison-Wesley Publishing, 1969.

Beckhard, Richard, and Harris, Reuben T. *Organizational Transitions: Managing Complex Change.* Reading, MA: Addison-Wesley Publishing Co., 1977.

Bennis, Warren G.; Benne, Kenneth D.; and Chin, Robert. *The Planning of Change.* 2d ed. New York: Holt, Rinehart and Winston, 1969.

Blake, Robert R., and Mouton, Jane S. *The Managerial Grid.* Houston, TX: Gulf Publishing Co., 1964.

Bommer, Michael R. W., and Chorba, Ronald W. *Decision Making for Library Management.* Professional Librarian Series. White Plains, NY: Knowledge Industry Publications, Inc., 1982.

Bommer, Michael R. W.; Chorba, Ronald W.; and Grattidge, Walter. *Decision Support Systems of the Academic Library.* Potsdam, NY: Clarkson College of Technology, 1980.

Bormann, Ernest G. *Discussion and Group Methods: Theory and Practice.* 2d ed. New York: Harper & Row, Publishers, 1975.

Bradford, Leland P.; Gibb, Jack R.; and Benne, Kenneth D., eds. *T-Group Theory and Laboratory Methods.* New York: John Wiley & Sons, Inc., 1964.

Buckley, Walter F., ed. *Modern Systems Research for the Behavioral Scientist.* Chicago: Aldine Publishing Company, 1968.

Campbell, Jeremy. *Grammatical Man.* New York: Simon and Schuster, 1982.

Cassata, Mary B., and Palmer, Roger Cain, eds. *Reader in Library Communication.* Englewood, CO: Information Handling Services, 1976.

Cohen, Harry. "The Tin Soldiers of Bureaucracy." *Management Review.* 61 (4) (April 1972): 3–9.

Conroy, Barbara. *Library Staff Development and Continuing Education: Principles and Practices.* Littleton, CO: Libraries Unlimited, Inc., 1978.

Dance, James C. "Public Relations for the Smaller Library." *Small Libraries Publication, No. 4* Chicago: Library Administration and Management Association, American Library Association, 1979, pp. 1–12.

De Bono, Edward. *New Think.* New York: Avon Books, 1971.

Dewey, John. *How We Think.* 2d ed. Boston: D. C. Heath and Company, 1933.

Dowlin, Kenneth E. *The Electronic Library.* New York: Neal-Schuman Publishers, Inc., 1984.

Drucker, Peter. Management Tasks, Responsibilities, Practices. New York: Harper & Row, 1974.

———. *Managing in Turbulent Times.* New York: Harper & Row, 1980.

———. *The Practice of Management.* New York: Harper & Row, 1954.

Eisenberg, Abne M. *Understanding Communication in Business and the Professions.* New York: Macmillan, 1978.

Emery, Richard. *Staff Communication in Libraries.* London: Clive Bingley, 1975.

Euster, Joanne R. "Changing Patterns in Communication in Large Academic Libraries." Occasional Paper, No. 6. Washington, DC: Association of Research Libraries, Office of Management Studies, 1981.

Farace, Richard V.; Monge, Peter R.; and Russell, Hamish M. *Communicating and Organizing.* Reading, MA: Addison-Wesley Publishing Co., 1977.

Fiedler, Fred E. *A Theory of Leadership Effectiveness.* New York: McGraw-Hill, 1967.

Finch, Frederic E.; Jones, Halsey R.; and Litterer, Joseph A. *Managing for Organizational Effectiveness: An Experiential Approach.* New York: McGraw-Hill, 1976.

Fournies, Ferdinand F. *Coaching for Improved Work Performance.* New York: Van Nostrand Reinhold Company, 1978.

Friedman, Selma. "Where Employees Go for Information (Some Surprises!)." *Administrative Management* 42 (9) (September 1981): 72–73.

Frost, Joyce Hocker, and Wilmot, William W. *Interpersonal Conflict.* Dubuque, IA: William C. Brown Company, Publishers, 1978.

Galbraith, Jay. *Organizational Design.* Reading, MA: Addison-Wesley, 1977.

Goldhaber, Gerald M. *Improving Institutional Communication.* New Directions for Institutional Advancement, No. 2. San Francisco, CA: Jossey-Bass, 1978.

Goldhaber, Gerald M. *Organizational Communication.* 2d ed. Dubuque, IA: William C. Brown Company, Publishers, 1979.

Goleman, Daniel. "The Electronic Rorschach." *Psychology Today* 17 (2) (February 1983): 36–43.

Golembiewski, Robert T. *Approaches to Planned Change.* Public Administration and Public Policy, No. 7. New York: Dekker, 1979.

Harnack, R. Victor; Fest, Thorrel B.; and Jones, Barbara Schindler. *Group Discussion: Theory and Technique* 2d ed. Englewood Cliffs, NJ: Prentice-Hall, Inc., 1977.

Havelock, Ronald G. *Planning for Innovation through Dissemination and Utilization of Knowledge.* Ann Arbor, MI: University of Michigan, Institute for Social Research, 1969.

Havelock, Ronald G., and Havelock, Mary C. *Training for Change Agents.* Ann Arbor, MI: University of Michigan, Institute for Social Research, 1973.

Herbert, Theodore T. *Organizational Behavior: Readings and Cases.* 2d ed. New York: Macmillan, 1981.

Hersey, Paul, and Blanchard, Kenneth. *Management of Organizational Behavior: Utilizing Human Resources.* 4th ed. Englewood Cliffs, NJ: Prentice-Hall, 1982.

Herzberg, Frederick. *Work and the Nature of Man.* Cleveland, OH: World Publishing, 1966.

Hunt, Gary T. *Communication Skills in the Organization.* Englewood Cliffs, NJ: Prentice-Hall, 1980.

Huse, Edgar, and Bowditch, James. *Behavior in Organizations.* Reading, MA: Addison-Wesley Publishing Co., 1973.

Huseman, Richard C., and Alexander, Elmore R., III. "Communication and the Managerial Function: A Contingency Approach." In *Organizational Behavior: Readings and Cases,* by Theodore T. Herbert. pp. 119–31. 2d ed. New York: Macmillan, 1981.

Huseman, Richard C.; Logue, Cal M.; and Freshley, Dwight L. *Readings in Interpersonal and Organizational Communication.* Boston: Allyn and Bacon, Inc., 1977.

Ilich, John, and Jones, Barbara Schindler. *Successful Negotiating Skills for Women.* Reading, MA: Addison-Wesley Publishing Company, 1980.

Janis, Irving L. "Groupthink." *Psychology Today* 5 (November 1971): 43–46i.

Jones, Barbara Schindler. *Written Communication for Today's Manager.* New York: Lebhar-Friedman Books, 1980.

Kanter, Rosabeth Moss. *The Change Masters.* New York: Simon and Schuster, 1983.

Kast, Fremont E., and Rosenzweig, James E. *Contingency Views of Organization and Management.* Chicago: Science Research Associates, Inc., 1973.

Klauss, Rudi, and Bass, Bernard M. *Interpersonal Communication in Organizations.* New York: Academic Press, 1982.

Kraus, William A. *Collaboration in Organizations: Alternatives to Hierarchy.* New York: Human Sciences Press, 1980.

Laborde, Genie Z. *Influencing with Integrity.* Palo Alto, CA: Syntony Publishing, 1984.

Lancaster, Wilfrid F., ed. *The Role of the Library in an Electronic Society.* Proceedings of the 1979 Clinic on Library Applications of Data Processing. Urbana-Champaign, IL: University of Illinois Graduate School of Library Science, 1980.

Lewis, Phillip V. *Organizational Communications: The Essence of Effective Management.* Columbus, OH: Grid, Inc., 1975.

Likert, Rensis. *New Patterns of Management.* New York: McGraw-Hill, 1961.

Likert, Rensis, and Likert, Jane Gibson. *New Ways of Managing Conflict.* New York: McGraw-Hill, 1976.

Locke, E. A. "Toward a Theory of Task Motivation and Incentives." *Organizational Behavior and Human Performance* 3 (2) (May 1968): 157–89.

Lucas, Henry C., Jr. *Information Systems Concepts for Managers.* New York: McGraw-Hill, 1977.

McClelland, David C. *The Achieving Society.* Princeton, NJ: D. Van Nostrand Co., 1961.

McClelland, David C., et al. *The Achievement Motive.* New York: Appleton-Century-Crofts, 1953.

McClure, Charles R. *Information for Academic Library Decision Making: The Case for Organizational Information Management.* Contributions in Librarianship and Information Science, No. 31. Westport, CT: Greenwood Press, 1980.

McDonald, Joseph. "Aspects of Management Information and Making Decisions." *Drexel Library Quarterly* 17 (2) (Spring 1981):61–76.

McGarry, Kevin J. *Communication Knowledge and the Librarian.* Hamden, CT: Linnet Books, 1975.

McGregor, Douglas. *The Human Side of Enterprise.* New York: McGraw-Hill, 1967.

———. *The Professional Manager.* New York: McGraw-Hill, 1967.

Marsh, Patrick O. *Messages that Work: A Guide to Communication Design.* Englewood Cliffs, NJ: Educational Technology Publications, 1983.

Maslow, A. H. *Motivation and Personality.* New York: Harper, 1954; revised 1970.

Massey, Morris. *The People Puzzle.* Reston, VA: Reston Publishing Company, Inc., 1979.

Mehrabian, Albert. *Public Places and Private Spaces: The Psychology of Work, Play and Living Environments.* New York: Basic Books, 1976.

Mella, Dorothee L. *Color Power: Your Personal Energy Resource.* Albuquerque, NM: Domel Artbooks, 1981.

Merry, Uri, and Allerhand, Melvin E. *Developing Teams and Organizations: A Practical Handbook for Managers and Consultants.* Reading, MA: Addison-Wesley Publishing Company, 1977.

Nadler, David A. *Concepts for Management of Organizational Change.* Research Working Paper 279A. New York: Columbia University, 1980.

Naisbitt, John. *Megatrends: Ten New Directions Transforming Our Lives.* New York: Warner Books, 1982.

Penland, Patrick R. *Communication for Librarians.* Pittsburgh, PA: University of Pittsburgh Bookstore, 1971. (preliminary edition)

Pfeiffer, William J., and Jones, John E. *The Annual Handbook for Group Facilitators.* La Jolla, CA: University Associates, Inc.

Powell, Judith W., and LeLieuvre, Robert B. *Peoplework: Communications Dynamics for Librarians.* Chicago: American Library Association, 1979.

Prather, Hugh. *A Book of Games: A Course in Spiritual Play* Garden City, NY: Doubleday & Company, Inc., 1981.

Pugh, D. S. ed. *Organization Theory.* New York: Penguin Books, 1971.

Rehnberg, Marilyn, ed. *Self Assessment Guide for Staff Communication.* St. Paul, MN: Office of Public Library and Interlibrary Cooperation, 1984.

Ries, Al, and Trout, Jack. *Positioning: The Battle for Your Mind.* New York: Warner Books, 1981.

Rizzo, John R. *Management for Librarians: Fundamentals and Issues.* Westport, CT: Greenwood Press, 1980.

Rogers, Carl. *On Becoming a Person.* Boston: Houghton Mifflin Company, 1961.

Rogers, Everett M., and Agarwala-Rogers, Rekha. *Communication in Organizations.* New York: Free Press, 1976.

Rogers, Everett M., and Kincaid, D. Lawrence. *Communication Networks: Towards a New Paradigm for Research.* New York: Free Press, 1981.

Rogers, Everett M., and Shoemaker, F. Floyd. *Communication of Innovations: A Cross-Cultural Approach.* New York: Free Press, 1971.

Schein, Edgar H. "Organizational Effectiveness." In *Behavioral Decisions in Organizations,* edited by Alvar Elbing, pp. 767–75. New York: Scott, Foresman and Co., 1970.

Schoch, Russell. "Checking Out the Library." *California Monthly* (March–April 1984): 15–17.

Shannon, Claude E., and Weaver, Warren. *The Mathematical Theory of Communication.* Urbana, IL: University of Illinois Press, 1949.

Sigel, Efrem. *Books, Libraries and Electronics: Essays on the Future of Written Communication.* White Plains, NY: Knowledge Industry Publications, 1982.

Skinner, B. F. *Beyond Freedom and Dignity.* New York: Alfred A. Knopf, 1971.

Smith, David. *Systems Thinking in Library and Information Management* New York: K. G. Saur, 1980.

Smith, H. T., and Green, T. R. G., eds. *Human Interaction with Computers.* New York: Academic Press, 1980.

Steinmetz, Lawrence L. *Interviewing Skills for Supervisory Personnel.* Reading, MA: Addison-Wesley Publishing Company, Inc., 1971.

Stewart, Charles J., and Cash, William B. *Interviewing: Principles and Practices.* Dubuque, IA: William C. Brown Company Publishers, 1974.

Stevens, Norman D. *Communication throughout Libraries.* Scarecrow Library Administration Series, No. 6. Metuchen, NJ: Scarecrow Press, 1983.

Stueart, Robert D., and Eastlick, John T. *Library Management.* Denver, CO: Libraries Unlimited, 1977.

Tague, Jean. "Computer Potential for Management Information." *Canadian Library Journal* 36 (5) (October 1979): 268–70.

Theobald, Robert. "The Future of the Librarian." *Public Libraries* 20 (3) (Fall 1981): p. 74–76.

Thompson, James C. "Advanced Library Obfuscation, or The Modifiable Ergonomic Dimensions of the English Language." *American Libraries* 15 (3) (March 1984): 138–42.

Timm, Paul R. *Functional Business Presentations.* Englewood Cliffs, NJ: Prentice-Hall, Inc., 1981.

Tortoriello, Thomas R.; Blatt, Stephen J.; and DeWine, Sue. *Communication in the Organization.* New York: McGraw-Hill, 1978.

Tuckman, B. W. "Developmental Sequence in Small Groups." *Psychological Bulletin* 63 (1965): 384–99.

Turner, Steve, and Weed, Frank. *Conflict in Organizations.* Englewood Cliffs, NJ: Prentice-Hall, Inc., 1983.

von Bertalanffy, Ludwig. "General System Theory—A Critical Review." In *Modern Systems Research for the Behavioral*

Scientist, edited by Walter Buckley, pp. 11–30. Chicago: Aldine Publishing Company, 1968.

von Oech, Roger. *A Whack on the Side of the Head.* New York: Warner Books, 1983.

Von Ward, Paul. *Dismantling the Pyramid.* Washington, DC: Delphi Press, 1981.

Vroom, Victor H. *Work and Motivation.* New York: John Wiley & Sons, 1964.

Wiener, Norbert. *Cybernetics: Or Control and Communication in the Animal and the Machine.* New York: John Wiley & Sons, 1948.

Wilkinson, J. P. "The Psycho-Organizational Approach to Staff Communication in Libraries." *The Journal of Academic Librarianship* 4 (1) (1978): 21–26.

Wonder, Jacquelyn, and Donavan, Priscilla. *Whole Brain Thinking: Working from Both Sides of the Brain to Achieve Peak Job Performance.* New York: William Morrow and Company, Inc., 1984.

Zand, Dale E. *Information, Organization, and Power: Effective Management in the Knowledge Society.* New York, McGraw-Hill, 1981.

Index

Compiled by Linda Webster